IZOBRAZITELNOYE ISKUSSTVO PUBLISHING HOUSE MOSCOW

STATE
ARMOURY
IN THE
MOSCOW
KREMLIN

IT WAS 1945, and winter was nearing its end. The blackout was still in force in Moscow, but on all sides there was a feeling of joy, a sense of the nearness of victory. All those things which in the dark days of retreat had been removed and hidden away in remote parts of the country—valuable museum exhibits, works of art and historical monuments—were being brought back to the capital.

At 7 a. m. on February 20, 1945, a long goods train pulled up at Kutuzovo Station, a few miles outside Moscow. It had brought the Kremlin Armoury exhibits back from safekeeping in the Urals. The boxes were unloaded with great care and delivered to the Kremlin, there to be taken up the white marble staircase of the Armoury. This marked the start of the work of which the staff had dreamt in those long and difficult days in the Urals. There was a great deal of re-thinking, the theme of the exhibition was decided upon and plans for setting out the collections were drawn up. As a result, the Armoury had all its exhibits on view before any of the other major museums of Europe.

The exhibition is arranged in nine halls. The first is devoted to ancient armour, accoutrements, firearms and cold steel. Some of the items on display are preserved as works of art made by the well-known Russian armourers Nikita Davydov, Dmitri Konovalov, Maxim Ivanov, Tretyak Pestrikov and Grigori Vyatkin, and others as objects of profound historical interest which had belonged to such outstanding Russian military leaders as Yermak (d. 1584), Dmitri Pozharsky (1578—1642) and Peter the Great (1671—1725), or captured on the battlefield: the Battle of Poltava (1709) or the Napoleonic War of 1812, and others as gifts from foreign states or merchants.

An exhibition of 10th—15th century gold and silver ware is laid out in the second hall. With a wealth of church plate, household utensils and magnificent jewelry, it gives a vivid idea of the variety of forms and ornamentation and of artistic techniques of metal-working.

In the third hall there is an unusual collection of Russian and foreign fabrics, old ecclesiastical vestments, and portrait and decorative embroidery dating back to the 12th century. Many of these works were made in the Moscow Kremlin. There are Russian embroidered icon-clothes, palls and shrouds, which are done in astonishingly beautiful colours and with great delicacy of taste. Decorative embroidery incorporating pearls and precious stones is especially well represented.

Objects from the workshops of the Cavalry Office are also widely represented. Two of the exhibition halls contain collections of ceremonial horse trappings—saddles, valuable harness and embroidered caparisons. Some of the finest craftsmen of the day worked on the trappings for the ceremonial processions, parades and hunts so popular in the 16th—17th centuries.

A considerable place is occupied by a collection of silverware by German, English and Dutch craftsmen and a unique collection of imperial regalia, thrones, crowns, sceptres, orbs and staffs.

Most of the Armoury's exhibits were made or acquired during the period when the Kremlin was the residence of the Grand Princes of Moscow, and later the tsars.

For centuries skilful craftsmen have worked at the Kremlin, first at the courts of the Grand Princes and metropolitans, and later at those of the tsars and patriarchs. Here new craftsmen were trained and master-craftsmen were brought from all over Russia, sometimes forcibly. The museum's collections tell the history of Russian decorative art in association with the activity of the workshops in the Kremlin grounds: the Armoury, the Silver and Gold Workshops, and those of the Tsar, the Tsarina, and the Cavalry Office.

The exhibits also include pieces of applied art from abroad which were in use at the Kremlin. A comparison of works produced in the West and in the Orient with those done by craftsmen and artists at the Kremlin emphasizes the original features and independent character of Russian decorative art and is an indication of the extent of the international links of the old Russian state.

What exactly were the workshops and vaults of the Kremlin, how and when did they come into being, why is a museum housing a rich variety of works of decorative and applied art called the Armoury, a name that does not suit its contents? It is not easy to answer these questions, for the documentary evidence extant is fragmentary and sometimes contradictory, and research is far from complete.

From the 14th century, when the power of the Moscow princes was established, there began a gradual accumulation of treasures which were concentrated in various storehouses in the Kremlin. In the wills of Moscow Prince Ivan Kalita (1325-41) and his successors there are lists of valuables: icons, vessels, arms, armour and clothing. The consistent efforts of the Grand Princes to unite Russian lands around Moscow, their successful fight for power with Novgorod and Tver, the continued strengthening of their economic position and finally the exceptional role played by Moscow in freeing the country from Tartar-Mongol oppression raised the status of the Moscow princes. In the 15th century Moscow became in fact the capital of the Russian lands. It grew rapidly in size and wealth. A tremendous amount of construction work was undertaken, and in 1485 a building was erected between the Cathedral of the Annunciation and the Archangel Michael Cathedral, and it was called the Treasury.

The first documentary record of the existence of the Armoury is in connection with the great fire of 1547, which reduced the Kremlin to ashes and destroyed many storehouses containing valuable works. "And there was a great storm... and the treasury of the great tsar was burnt down, and the Armoury was burnt with all military weapons, and the Household Chamber with its storehouse was all burnt; everything that was of wood in the cellars of the tsar's court beneath the chamber was burnt, and also the tsar's stables."

Along with the Armoury the chronicle mentions the Household Chamber, the tsar's stables and the tsar's treasury.

There exist documents and accounts by foreigners giving an idea of the extent of the immense wealth concentrated in the Kremlin in the 16th century. In February

1572 valuables from the Tsar's Treasury arrived in Novgorod, having been sent out of Moscow because of the danger of another invasion by the Crimean Tartars. Altogether 450 sledges were required to transport them. Foreign envoys Kobenzel, Varkoc and Horsey remarked upon the unparalleled luxury of the tsar's apparel, the sumptuous furnishing of the palace and the abundance of valuable plate on the festive board.

The intensification of feudal oppression in the latter half of the 16th century, along with the extension of trading ties and the consolidation of Russian state centralisation made for a still greater accumulation of treasure at the Kremlin. At the end of the 16th century a point was made of showing eminent foreigners the contents of the Treasury. Margeret, a Frenchman who was chief of the body-guard of Dmitri, the First Pretender, gave a vivid account of this storehouse: "In the Treasury I saw about fifty robes of the tsar decorated with embroidery in valuable materials instead of braid; I saw garments covered with pearls from neck to hem, or with pearl-encrusted borders of a foot or from four to six inches all round; half a dozen covers, pearl-encrusted, and other such things. They also have there extremely valuable gems which are bought every year, apart from those presented by envoys from abroad; there are four crowns, three for tsars and a fourth for one of the old Grand Princes, apart from one that was started but not altogether completed, for the tsarina of tsar Dmitri ... two sceptres and two gold orbs". Margeret was highly impressed with the abundance of gold vessels of various sizes and the "infinite multitude" of silver plate made by Russian masters. He remarked particularly on the immense number of German, English and Polish utensils brought to the tsar by foreign envoys or purchased because of their rarity, and the mass of precious velvets, brocades and silks.

When Dmitri the Pretender acceded to the throne on June 20, 1605, he began to plunder these treasures, and by 1612 the Kremlin and its storehouses had been devastated to an appalling degree.

After the interventionists had been driven out of Moscow an energetic start was made on the restoration of the Kremlin and its riches. The first of the Romanovs did everything he could to make good the losses, and the main source for this, as in the past, was the imposition of a poll tax. Russian envoys and merchants who went abroad or to border regions were instructed to bring back for the tsar's treasury precious stones and fabrics, gold and silver plate and other goods "suitable for the state treasury".

By the end of the 1620s a unique collection of silver had been built up in Moscow. In 1628 some extremely rare silver plate was acquired in Archangel from the treasure stores of King Christian IV of Denmark. It included work done by the famous German goldsmiths Christophe Jamnitzer, Jacob Mores the Elder and Heinrich Bordeslow. A year later Fabian Ulyanov, the commercial agent for England, delivered a new consignment of silver to the Kremlin, including some world-famous sculptural vessels in the form of leopards. Not long after the expulsion of the interventionists the art workshops of the Kremlin were revived. The biggest of these

I. THE ARMOURY (BUILT 1851). ARCHITECT K. A. TON (1794—1881). DETAIL OF FAÇADE

was the Armoury, where craftsmen proficient in many trades worked on the making and repair of firearms, cold steel and armour. The finest of the craftsmen were entrusted with the task of making ceremonial arms for the tsar. Among the master craftsmen at the Armoury during the first half of the century were painters and icon painters, who in addition to decorating standards, tents and ensigns had to paint icons and frescoes for cathedrals and churches and embellish the palaces and storehouses. At that time the Armoury was quite near the Trinity Gate of the Kremlin, housed on the upper two floors of a large building opposite the Poteshny Palace. The vaulted ceiling and walls were decorated with frescoes and purely ornamental painting. Part of it was set aside for the most valuable weapons; here stood coffers for richly decorated arms of high artistic value, made by Russian armourers or brought from abroad.

The Gold and Silver Halls stood by the Armoury, and it was here that astoundingly beautiful and sumptuous crowns, jewellery, valuable plate and sacred objects were made by enamellers, chasers and experts in niello and filigree work.

In the 17th century the Tsar's and Tsarina's Workshops were of particular importance. Founded, no doubt, originally as a offshoot of the Household Chamber, which is mentioned in 16th century documents, they made clothes for the tsar and his family. Their craftsmen did splendid embroidery, made lace of great value and unique shrouds and palls. The artistic portrait and decorative embroidery

II. THE ARMOURY (BUILT 1851). ARCHITECT K. A. TON. VIEW FROM BOLSHOI KAMENNY BRIDGE

which was so magnificently developed in the Kremlin workshops in itself constitutes a wonderful branch of old Russian art. In the western part of the Kremlin grounds, near the Borovitsky Gate, stood the Cavalry Office, on the spot where the Armoury stands today. It was responsible for the extensive royal stables, for the use of horses and carriages for ceremonial occasions, for making saddles, harnesses, caparisons and other horse-cloths and the safekeeping of all that was in the Cavalry Treasury. In addition to an equerry, clerks, stewards, and other attendants and grooms, the Cavalry Office employed saddlers, harness-makers and coach and carriage builders.

As a result of the work of the Cavalry Office, the museum has an unusual collection of objects from the Cavalry Treasury, either made at the Kremlin or brought to Moscow by envoys from Persia, Turkey, Denmark, China and other countries in the 16th and 17th centuries.

All these Kremlin workshops reached their peak in the second half of the 17th century. Historians investigating the development of the workshops compare them to an Academy of Arts, for "the influence of the Kremlin masterpieces extended throughout the Russian lands... over a period of many years the Kremlin gathered together the principal creative forces of the country. With them they brought their ability, their working habits, and their determination to engage in hard work to create art of a high order" (M. V. Alpatov).

IX

By the end of the 17th century a number of the Kremlin workshops were producing considerably less than before, and in 1699 the Tsar's and Tsarina's Workshops were amalgamated. In 1700 the Gold and Silver Halls were abolished and their artists and craftsmen transferred to the Armoury.

In 1709 the Armoury received a great many trophies from the Battle of Poltava: weapons, standards and personal belongings of King Charles XII of Sweden (1682-1718). In the second decade of the 18th century the Armoury ceased to be a workshop, and in 1711 the finest of the Kremlin's masters were sent to St Petersburg. Vast quantities of historic valuables gathered from the vaults of the workshop offices: the Armoury, the Treasury, the Cavalry Treasury—were transferred to the new Treasury, and one person was entrusted with the stewardship of the combined storehouse, from then on known as the Workshop and Armoury. Before the end of the 18th century the collection was several times moved to different places, as the dark, dank rooms of the Kremlin buildings were altogether unfit for the storage of these treasures amassed over the centuries. Furthermore, high officials of state helped themselves to works of art in great numbers, and it was only at the beginning of the 19th century that some steps were taken to convert this unique collection into a museum. In 1804 and 1805 a complete inventory was made, and in 1807 the first printed work on the history of the Armoury was published, under the title "Historical Description of the Armoury". In 1820 a special building was at last constructed near the Trinity Gate to designs prepared by architect I. V. Yegotov (1756—1815). In view of the approach of the enemy army in 1812, the Armoury treasures had been removed to Nizhny-Novgorod two days before the Battle of Borodino, and when they were brought back to Moscow they were set out immediately in the five halls of the new museum. In 1835 Ushakov, the director of the museum, and his staff drew up a list of the entire contents of the Workshop and Armoury—the "Archive of the State Museum of the Moscow Kremlin".

In the first half of the 19th century the Armoury acquired some exhibits that were subsequently to become world-famous. There were a magnificent gold yoke and other decorations from the Staro-Ryazan treasure, the helmet of Prince Yaroslav Vsevolodovich of Pereslavl-Zalessky, weapons belonging to Kozma Minin (d. 1616), leader of the people's militia in 1612, to D. M. Pozharsky and others. Two collectors, M. P. Pogodin (1800-75) and P. F. Korabanov (1767—1851), handed over their own collections of works of art to be added to the exhibits.

When the Grand Kremlin Palace was being constructed in the middle of the 19th century a new Armoury building was erected in the western part of the Kremlin grounds, near the Borovitsky Gate, the architect for which was K. A. Ton (1794—1881). All the exhibits were moved there in 1851 and housed in two high-ceilinged halls on the first floor. Two halls on the ground floor were intended for the valuable old documents of the Armoury archives. In 1856 the archives were put in the charge of F. A. Filimonov (1812-98) who later became assistant director of the Armoury, and he made a vital contribution to research on the history of the Armoury exhibits. He was asked in 1867 to prepare an exhibition of old

Russian art for display in France, and works from the Armoury occupied a prominent place in it. The exhibition made a tremendous impression in Paris, arousing great interest in the culture of the Russian people.

Filimonov was an artist, archeologist and historian and was outstanding as a museum curator; he performed a great service in compiling the first scientific inventory of the Armoury, an undertaking in which V. Yakovlev and Chaev also took

III. INTERIOR OF THE ARMOURY. WHITE-MARBLE STAIRCASE

part. The noteworthy feature of this many-volume work was that it combined detailed descriptions of items, which included facsimiles of hallmarks and old inscriptions on objects, and valuable extracts from ancient accounts, records and the inventory books of the tsar's treasury in the 12th century. This "Inventory of the Armoury", published between 1884 and 1893, is still of scientific value today, and at the time it was the finest example of its kind to be produced by any museum at home or abroad. During the latter part of the century some well-known historians were working at the Armoury: S. M. Soloviev (1820-79), I. E. Zabelin (1820—1908) and A. A. Viktorov, and the museum's reputation grew steadily. In 1914-5, when the First World War broke out, valuables were brought to the Kremlin from the Winter Palace and the Hermitage in Leningrad, from the tsar's estate in Byelovezhsky Forest, and other places thought to be in danger.

Right up to the Socialist Revolution in October 1917 the Armoury continued to be in the nature of a purely court museum under the constant supervision and petty XI tutelage of the Royal Ministry. This affected the character of the exhibition for side by side with masterpieces of unique historical and artistic value were objects without the slightest value but included because they had some connection or other with the tsar's family.

After the October Revolution the character of the Armoury underwent a thorough and fundamental change.

The last shots of the Revolution were still echoing in the streets of Moscow when a body set up by the Moscow Soviet, the Commission for the Preservation of Artistic and Historic Monuments, started work in the Kremlin.

By an order issued by A. V. Lunacharsky (1875—1933), People's Commissar for Education, everything then in the Kremlin —"buildings, artistic and historical monuments, regardless of their ownership or use by any institution, including churches, cathedrals and monasteries"...—was declared the property of the Republic. In the early months after the Revolution various valuables from confiscated private collections and certain museums were temporarily stored in the Armoury. When the Soviet Government moved to Moscow in 1918 the efforts under way to preserve works of artistic and historical value received direct support from Lenin. Contemporary documents and eye-witness accounts emphasize that, although he was tremendously busy, Lenin found time to give orders for the restoration of the Nikolsky Gate, to take an interest in the progress of work on the Cathedral of the Dormition and to visit the Armoury to make certain that things were being properly looked after.

At the Eighth Congress of the Communist Party of the Soviet Union a decision was taken to "open up and make accessible to the working people all the art treasures which have been created by exploiting their labour and have hitherto been exclusively at the disposal of the exploiters". Consequent upon this treasures from the vaults of the Patriarch and masterpieces hidden away in the vaults of the Kremlin cathedrals and churches began to be handed over to the Armoury; its collections thus became highly comprehensive and it gained in significance.

The basis of the present exhibition is provided by works of art which were produced in the Kremlin's workshops and have lain in its coffers for centuries. Since the chronological principle is strictly adhered to, it is possible to follow trends of development of applied art in old Russia.

An astonishing number of the exhibits are unique. They are not coldly ranged round on shelves as in so many museums. Rather, the abundance of exhibits has made it possible to arrange them in more or less natural groups. No other collection has been amassed in such a way as this, independently of the vagaries of the tastes and incomes of private collectors.

The interesting thing about the collection is that the objects in it were made for use and those who made them saw their work fulfilling its function in churches, palaces and during various ceremonies.

Today these works of art live on right there in the Kremlin where they were made
XII and have reposed for so long. Their beauty and their close association with major

IV. INTERIOR OF THE ARMOURY. VIEW OF THE SECOND FLOOR HALLS OF THE EXHIBITION

The silver pieses usually bear designs of birds, flowers, representations of the Tree of Life and saints. Similar silver decorations are used on the epitrachelion and the wrist-bands which were once the property of the Metropolitan Alexius. From the mid-fourteenth century, in the wake of the process of unification of the Russian lands around Moscow the level of artistic handicraft work began to improve. This was due to the general upsurge of Russian culture resulting from the economic and political upsurge within the country. Moscow began to gather together artists and handicraftsmen acquainted with old techniques and traditions. At the end of the fourteenth century Moscow art emerged with its own artistic variation of Russian art. In the latter half of the fifteenth century Moscow developed and attained importance as a state, the power of the Grand Prince increased; Moscow became a wealthy state, which led to palace and court life achieving a high degree of sophisticated elegance and luxury. A number of art workshops were set up at the court of the Grand Prince to manufacture arms and gold and silver ware. Applied art attained great dignity and richness.

In the sixteenth century local schools of art began to lose their independent importance and were assimilated into the Moscow school, which developed into a general Russian style.

One can judge the height of artistic culture in old Russia from these works of twelfth-fifteenth century art in the Armoury collectio. They feature unique national characteristics and enable one to see the ancient foundations of the applied art of many ancient Russian centres: Kiev, Vladimir, Suzdal, Staraya Ryazan, Pereslavl-Zalessky, Novgorod, Pskov, Tver and Moscow.

1. HELMET OF PRINCE YAROSLAV VSEVOLODOVICH OF PERESLAVL-ZALESSKY. LATE 12TH—EARLY 13TH CENTURY. DETAIL

2. HELMET OF PRINCE YAROSLAV VSEVOLODOVICH OF PERESLAVL-ZALESSKY. LATE 12TH—EARLY 13TH CENTURY ▶

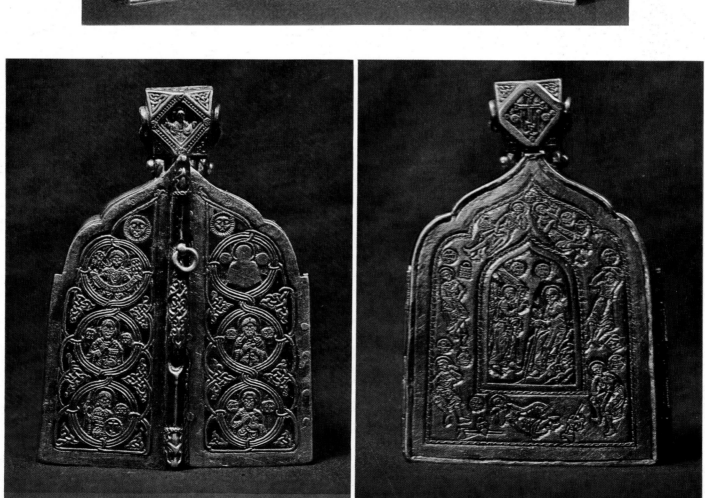

3. "BARMY" OF GRAND PRINCES. 12TH—13TH CENTURY

4. SMALL ICON "ST DEMETRIUS OF THESSALONICA". 13TH—14TH CENTURY

5, 6, 7.   TRIPTYCH. MADE BY LUCIAN. 1412

8.   HELMET WITH IRON-CLAD NECKLACE. 14TH CENTURY ▶

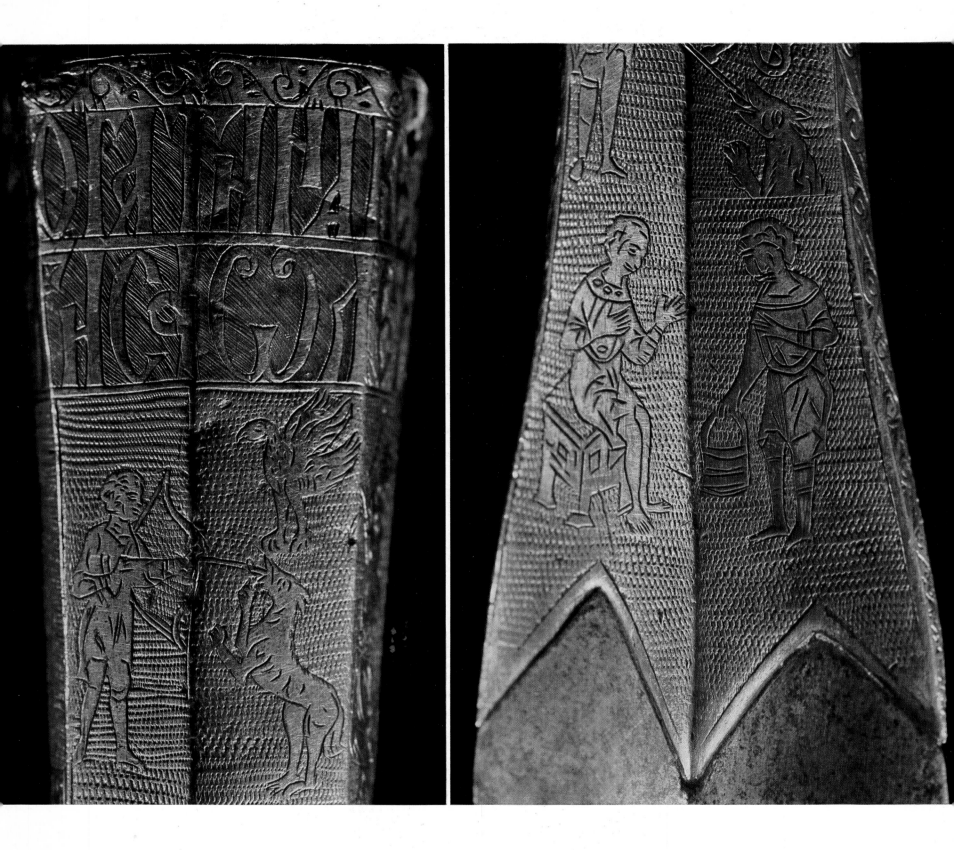

9, 10.   BOAR-SPEAR OF TVER PRINCE BORIS ALEXANDROVICH. 15TH CENTURY. DETAILS
11.   BOAR-SPEAR OF TVER PRINCE BORIS ALEXANDROVICH ▶

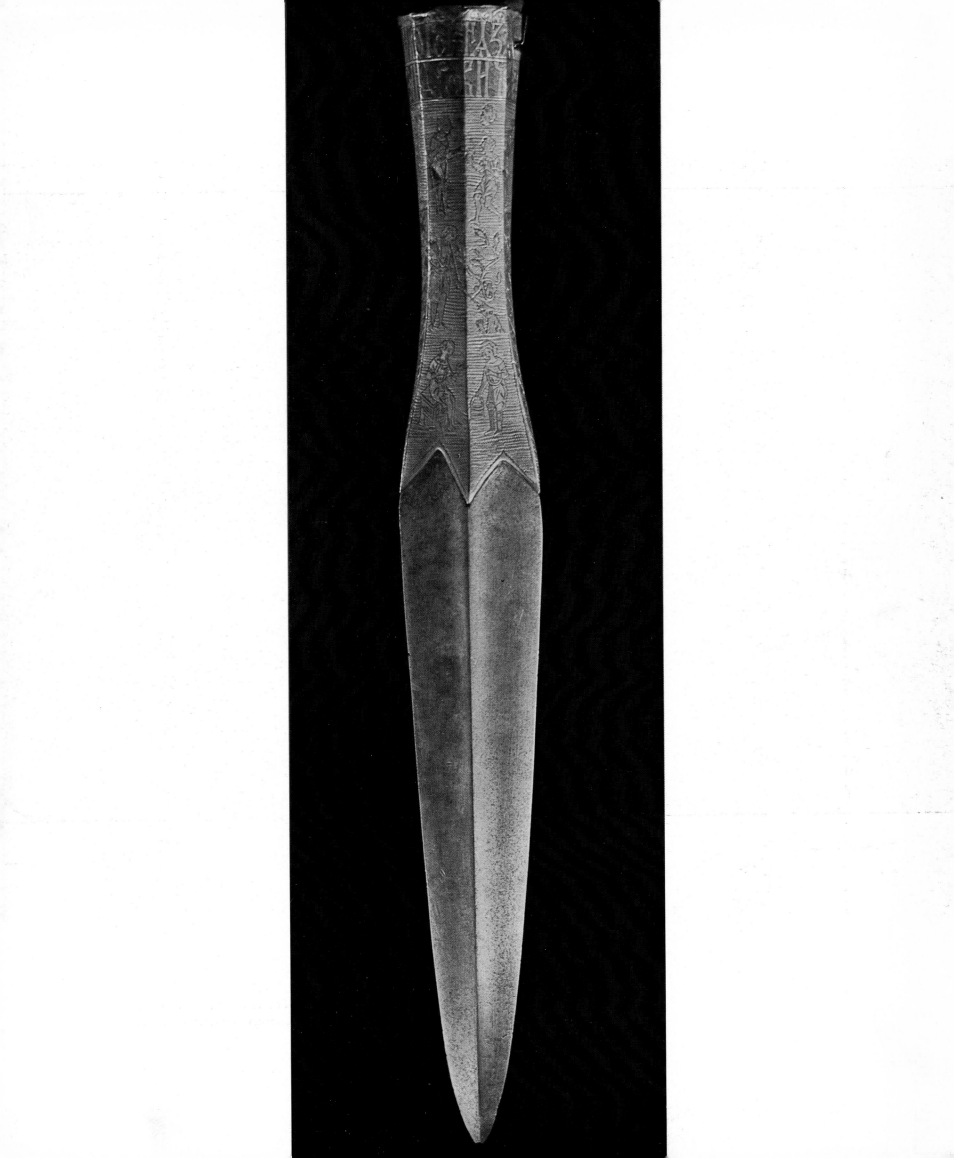

12. MOUNTING OF ICON "THE VIRGIN OF VLADIMIR". 13TH CENTURY. DETAIL
13. CHALICE OF PRINCE YURI DOLGORUKY. MID-12TH CENTURY ▶

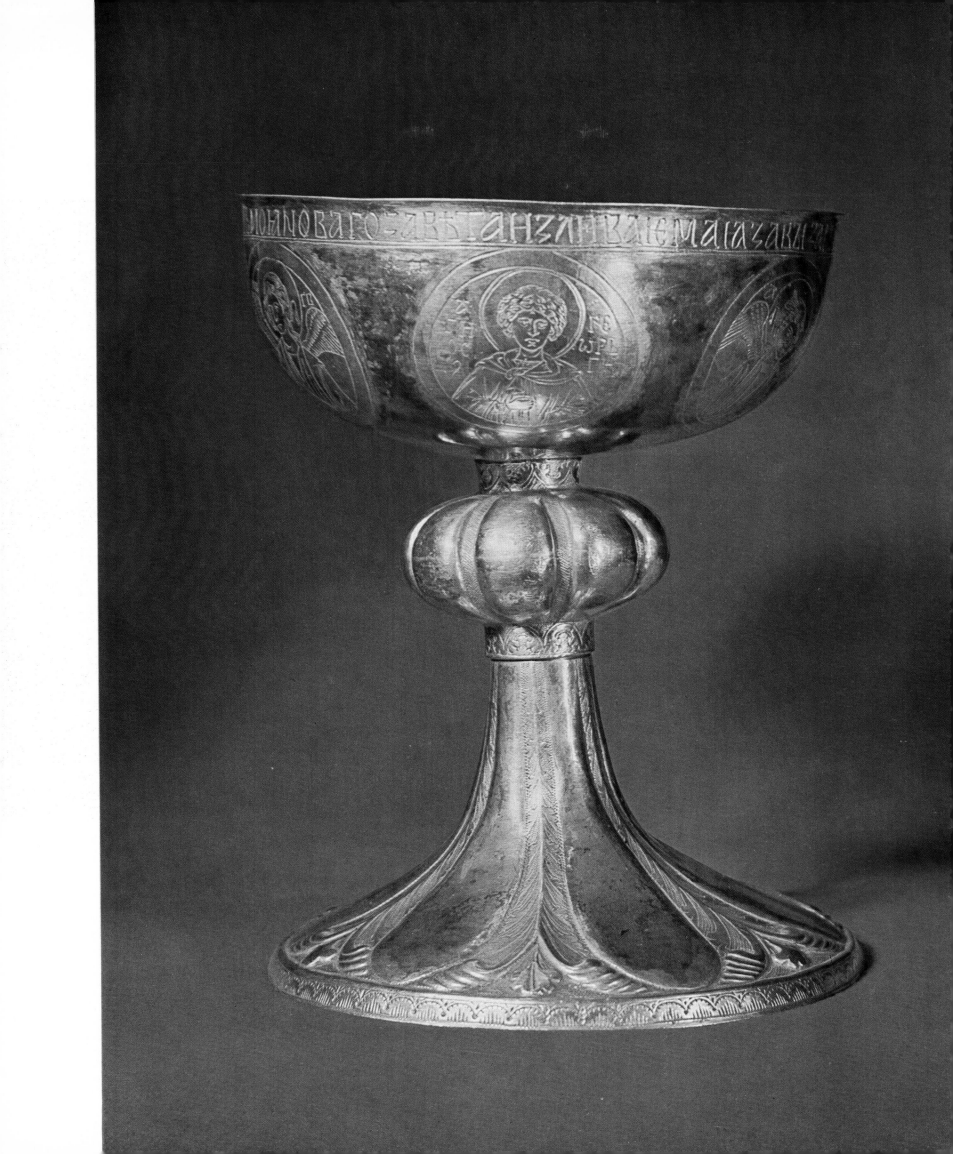

14. GREAT ZION. 1486. DETAIL

15. GREAT ZION ▶

16, 17. ICON "THE VIRGIN ELEUSA". 14TH CENTURY MOUNTING. 18TH-CENTURY ICON-PAINTING

18. CENSER OF PRINCE YURI VASSILIEVICH. 1469

19. PANAGIA. 15TH CENTURY ▶

20. CHALICE OF ARCHBISHOP MOSES OF NOVGOROD. 1329 ▶

21. GOSPELS OF METROPOLITAN SIMON OF MOSCOW. COVER. 1499. DETAIL
22. GOSPELS OF METROPOLITAN SIMON OF MOSCOW.   COVER. 1499 ▶

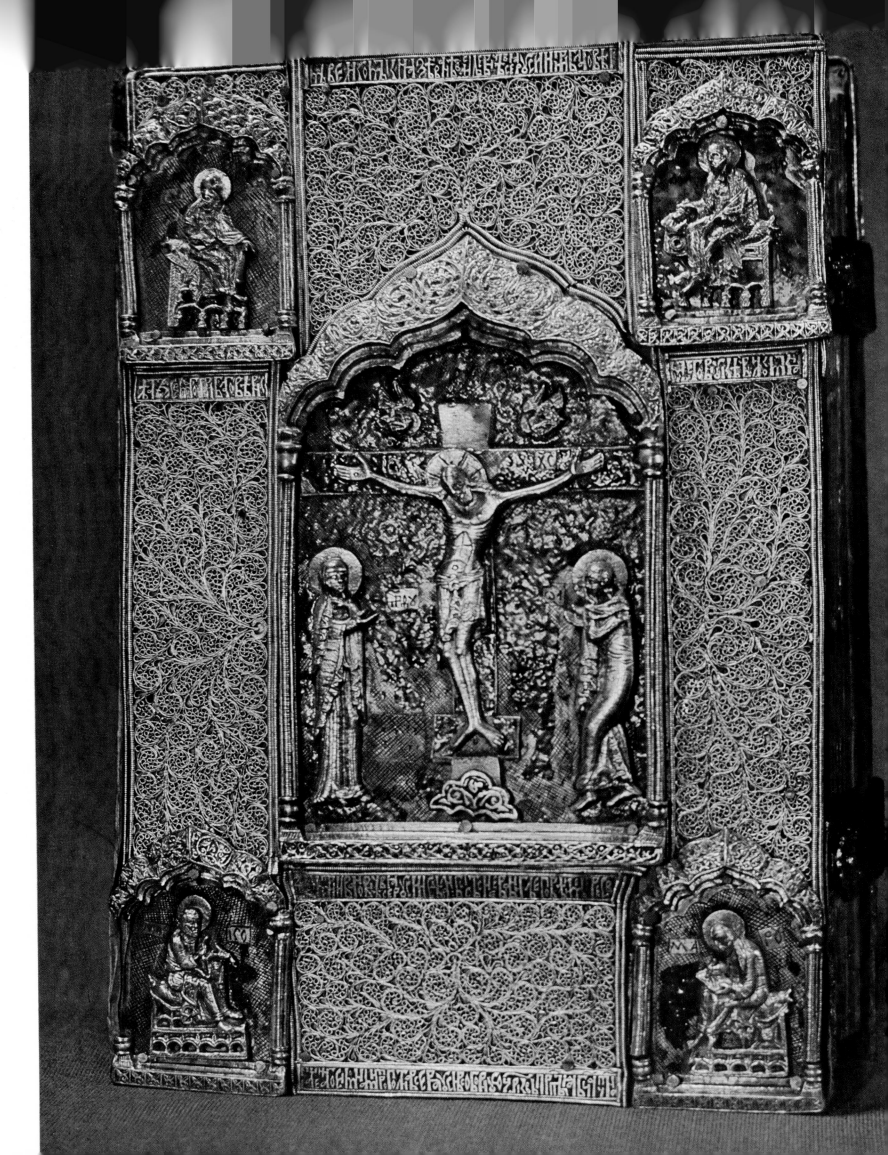

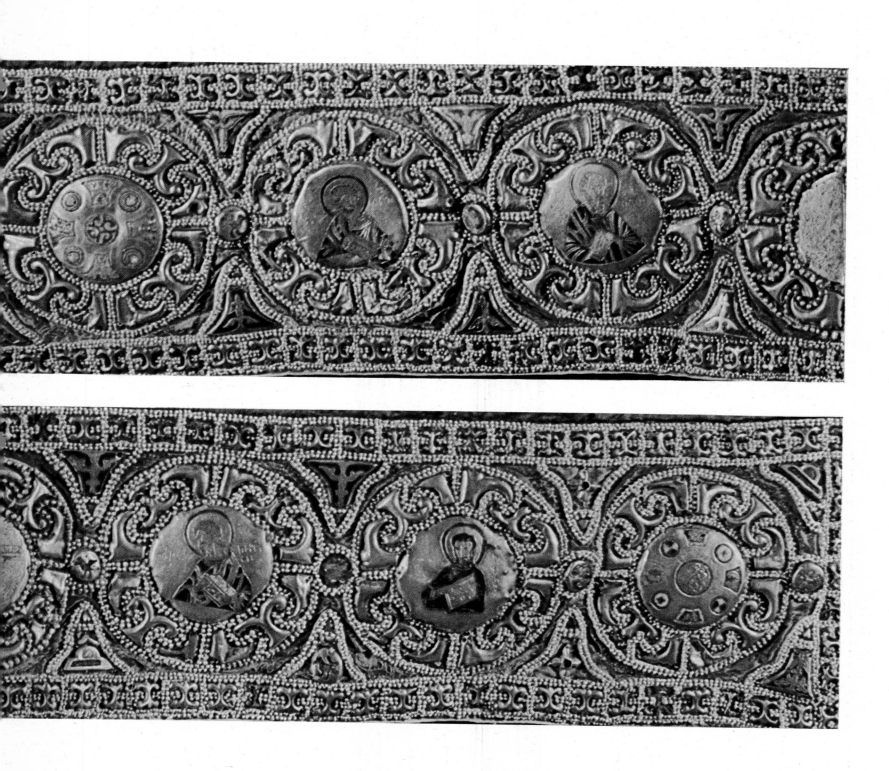

23, 24. SAKKOS OF METROPOLITAN ALEXIUS OF MOSCOW. SLEEVES. 1364
25. SAKKOS OF METROPOLITAN ALEXIUS OF MOSCOW. 1364 ▶

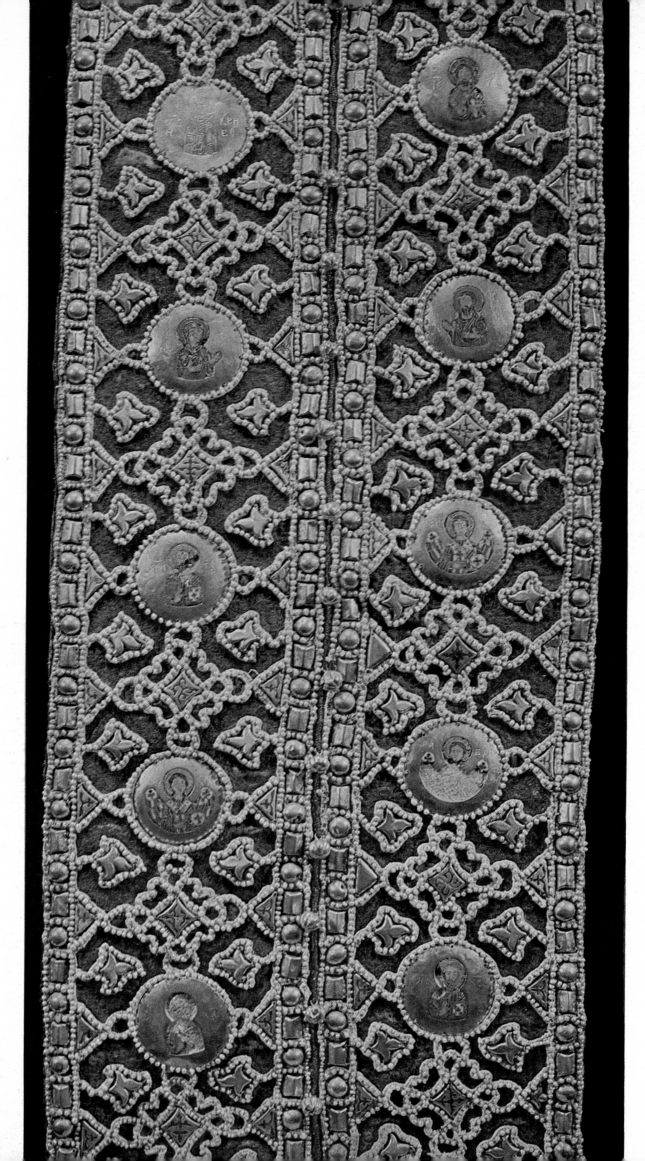

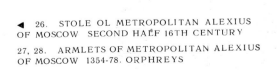

26. STOLE OL METROPOLITAN ALEXIUS
OF MOSCOW SECOND HALF 16TH CENTURY

27, 28. ARMLETS OF METROPOLITAN ALEXIUS
OF MOSCOW 1354-78. ORPHREYS

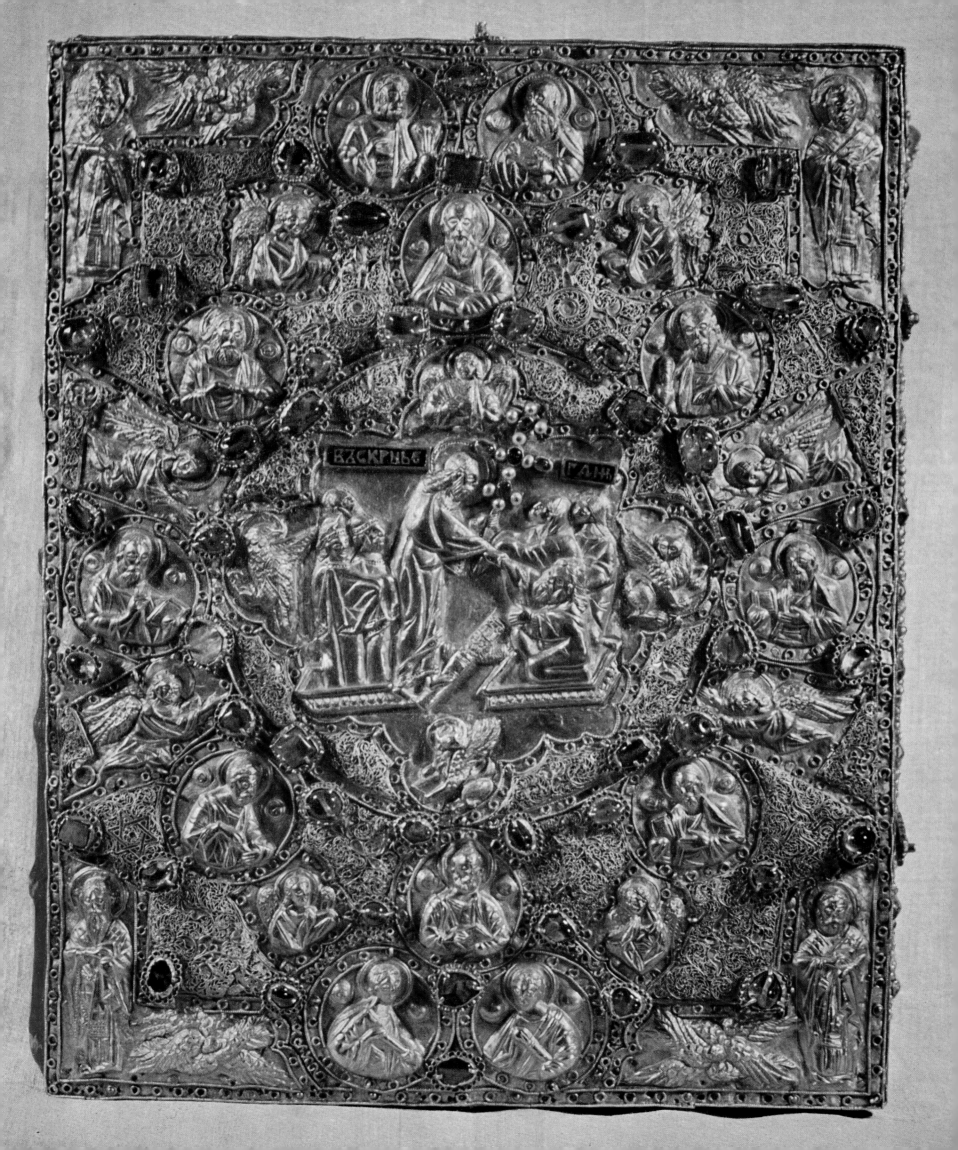

ЪНАЧАЛАБЕСЛО
ВО.ИСЛОВОБЕКЪ
БОЦ.ИБЪБЕ
СЛОВО.СЕБЕ
ИСКОНИВЪБЕ ВЬ
САТЕЦЬБЫША. И
БЕЗНЕГОННЧЕСОЖЕ
НЕБЫ.ЕЖЕБЫ ВЬТ
ЦЬЖИВОТЪБЕ.ИМЖІ

БІТЪБЕСВЕТЧЛО
ВЕКОЦЬ.ИСВЕТЬ
ВЬТЦЕСВЕТИТСА
ИТЬЦАЕГОНЕОБЬЦ
ТЪ.БЫЧЛВКЪПОСЛ
НЬЮБА.НИЖЕЦОЦ
ИОЛИНЬ.СЕПРИИДЕ
ВЬСВИДЕТЕЛЬСТВО
ДАСВИДЕТЕЛЬСТВОЦ

31. "MOROZOV" GOSPELS. MINIATURE. FIRST THIRD 15TH CENTURY

32. "MOROZOV" GOSPELS. MINIATURE. FIRST THIRD 15TH CENTURY

33. PUCHEZHA SHROUD OF CHRIST. 1441. ▶

ДМНТР

34, 35. SHROUD "ST DEMETRIUS OF THESSALONICA". 15TH CENTURY

BYZANTINE ART
OF THE
5-15 th
CENTURIES

THE COLLECTION of masterpieces of Byzantine applied art at the State Armoury is of great artistic and historical value despite its comparatively small size. It comprises splendid rare Byzantine cameos in the form of various small icons and panagias in gold settings (the settings were often made by Russian master craftsmen) with further embellishments of precious stones, and gold, silver and *cloisonné* objects and liturgical robes.

This interesting collection is not well known even among specialists. It was accumulated in the course of centuries and is entirely different in character from other collections. Many of the items were especially made in Byzantium as gifts for Russian rulers and various historical figures and were in the possession of Russian Grand Princes and church dignitaries.

After the Great October Socialist Revolution when all the Kremlin treasures stored were proclaimed state property and later founded the basis of the collections of the Kremlin museums, objects of Byzantine art were found among them. For instance, after 1918 the Armoury received sakkoses of the Russian Metropolitans Peter, Photius and Simon, an eleventh century reliquary, pectoral icons, panagias and other objects of Byzantine applied art.

Associated with certain historical events of our state or with individual political and ecclesiastical figures, these objects are evidence of the longstanding economic, political and cultural ties between old Russia and Byzantium. At the same time they are first-class works of art and give some idea of handicrafts in Byzantium.

There were all kinds of craftsmen in the court workshops in Constantinople: some worked in metal, some in stone or bone carving and a particular speciality was the production of precious silk and woolen cloth.

The numerous artistic works made at the court workshops (the trade secrets were cautiously guarded) were used mainly for decorating the churches and palaces of the nobility and the Emperor and for making the court ceremonies, which were famous throughout the medieval world for their magnificence and brilliance, even more elegant and sophisticated.

Developing as it did for over a thousand years, from the fourth to the fifteenth centuries, Byzantine art traversed a complex and unique road. The artistic culture of Byzantium which assimilated the heritage of Greek antiquity and the traditions of the ancient Orient, and which evolved its own style over a long period was at a far higher level of development than those of Western Europe. An essential role in its formation and development was played by the Slavs, who populated a considerable territory of the Balkans and Asia Minor and who had their own well developed artistic culture.

The fourth and fifth centuries could be called pre-Byzantine. The artistic traditions of late antiquity art had a strong influence, as can be seen in the figures of the Muses on the late fourth or early fifth century silver ewer from the Sudzhensky treasure. The frontal poses of the Muses facing the viewer, the tendency towards two-dimensional representation, the movement of their bodies and slight inclination of their heads towards the shoulder, the placing of the feet, their hair styles, the ornamentation of their garments and other details are characteristic both of late Roman and early Byzantine art.

The State Armoury has no objects of sixth-ninth century Byzantine art in its collection.

The ninth and tenth centuries are popularly known as the period of the Macedonian Renaissance after the name of the ruling dynasty of Byzantine Emperors. This was the time when lively trade, political and cultural relations between Byzantium and Russia came into being as is witnessed by the signing of various trade agreements and the establishment of regular diplomatic relations and the introduction of Christianity to Russia.

In the Armory collection this period is represented by a number of first-class cameos ("Christ Blessing" and other small icons, and a reliquary).

During the eleventh-twelfth century period, known to historians as the Comnenian after the ruling Comnenian dynasty, Byzantine art reached its peak. It was in this period that a dignified and elevated style consonant with the ideology of feudal society became firmly established.

This period is represented in the collection of the Armoury by a number of superior cameos and objects executed in the *cloisonné* technique. An especially interesting one is a carved steatite icon depicting the equestrian figure of St Demetrius of Thessalonica and bearing witness to the Byzantine master craftsman's worderful ability to create an impression of grandeur and solemnity even in a small work of art. Legend has it that the icon was a gift from a Byzantine Emperor to the Grand Prince Dmitri Donskoi (1350—89) of Moscow as a memento and blessing in connection with the 1380 victory on Kulikovo Field.

The heroic images of SS Demetrius and George, two warrior saints and martyrs, can be seen on many objects. Their cult was well known both in Byzantium and Georgia and later in Western Europe and old Russia. The Cathedral of St Demetrius in Thessalonica was known in Russia. One of the items in the collection, the eleventh century silver reliquary, is supposed to be a scale model of the cathedral and is a remarkable and rare work of Byzantine silverware.

The supreme achievement of applied art is the famous Byzantine enamel work represented by small gold items with the image of the Crucifixion and the Anastasis. One of them, an oval icon, was a part of the 1822 Staro-Ryazan treasure. On such icons the enamel is of superior quality. Byzantine enamels, which were always famous for their exceptional finesse, greatly influenced enamel workmanship in other countries, for example, they were particularly widely known in Kievan Rus. Enamel work was used in Byzantium for embellishments of the Emperor's robes and the vestments of high ecclesiastics, and for crowns, cups, dishes, crosses and reliquaries used on state occasions.

The final resurgence of Byzantine art is usually referred to as the Paleologos Renaissance. It found its finest expression in painting and in some techniques of applied art: metalwork and embroidery and the manufacture of rich textiles.

One of the items of the collection is a helmet with the Deesis which from iconographic evidence appears to have been made in the latter half of the thirteenth century and was quite possibly the property of the Paleologos Emperors. Later it found its way to the treasury of the Russian Grand Princes when Sophia Paleologos, a Byzantine Princess who was the second wife of the Grand Prince Ivan III (1462—1505) of Moscow, came to Moscow.

Up to the mid-fifteenth century Byzantine fabrics were widely used in Russia. The Armoury collection has two sakkoses in the group of Byzantine textiles which, according to the earliest inventory of the Patriarch's vaults, taken in 1631, belonged to the Metropolitan Photius.

Of great interest and exceptional artistic importance are also the sakkoses of the Russian Metropolitans Peter and Simon. Made in the court workshops of Constantionople from valuable Byzantine textiles, the sakkoses are decorated with magnificent artistic embroidery in silk, gold and pearls.

The sakkos of Peter, first Metropolitan of Moscow (1308-26), was made in 1322 from light blue silk satin and has a pattern of stripes of roundels with gold crosses. Such "cross" textiles were specially manufactured for the vestments of high priests.

The two sakkoses of Photius (1409-31), the Metropolitan of Moscow, are examples of splendidly skilful portrait embroidery. The embroidery of the "Minor" sakkos, despite the abundance of gold and silver, is outstanding for its bright colour, which brings it close to painting. The "Major" sakkos, in addition to its magnificent embroidery, is interesting for the fact that besides the portraits of the Byzantine Emperor and his wife it has portraits of Grand Prince Vassili Dmitrievich of Moscow and his wife, Sophia Witowtovna. This is a sign not only of the deep political and cultural ties which existed between Russia and Byzantium but of the growing strength and authority of the Moscow state, whose support the Byzantine Emperor was seeking during a period fraught with difficulty for the Byzantine Empire. Many eleventh-fifteenth century Byzantine gold and silver works are decorated with chasing, *repoussé* or filigree. Most of them are ornamented with intertwined floral patterns.

One of the most magnificent works of early fifteen century Byzantine filigree is the gold mounting for the icon of the Virgin of Vladimir made to the order of the Metropolitan Photius. Amidst the very fine filigree ornamentation of the mounting are bas-relief chased representations of the Church Feasts, the composition being somewhat crude and uninteresting despite a high degree of technical skill. This indicates a certain artistic decline in Byzantine art of the period.

While Byzantine art was declining, Moscow art was flourishing. Russian master craftsmen, assimilating the best of Byzantine culture which suited their demands and tastes, at the same time evolved their own distinct artistic style.

In 1453 Constantinople was captured by the Turks, and the Byzantine Empire fell. Though Byzantium perished as an independent state, its mighty, well developed rich artistic culture played a very important role in the history of world culture. For the art of the Slav people, the Russians above all, Byzantine culture was of immense importance.

36. HELMET WITH THE DEESIS. 13TH CENTURY. DETAIL
37. HELMET WITH THE DEESIS. 13TH CENTURY ▶

38, 39, 40, 41. EWER.
C. 400 A.D.

42. ICON "CHRIST BLESSING". 10TH-CENTURY CAMEO. 15TH-CENTURY SETTING. RUSSIA

43. ICON "CHRIST BLESSING". 10TH-CENTURY CAMEO. 15TH-CENTURY SETTING. RUSSIA

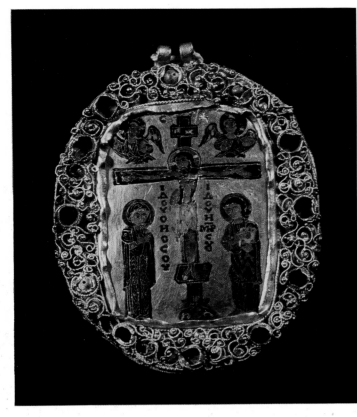

44. SMALL ICON "CRUCIFIXION WITH INTERCEDING SAINTS".
11TH CENTURY. 12TH—13TH CENTURY SETTING. KIEVAN RUS

45. SMALL ICON-RELIQUARY "THE DESCENT INTO HELL". 12TH CENTURY

46. PHILOTHEUS' STAUROTHÈQUE. 12TH CENTURY   47. ICON "ST DEMETRIUS OF THESSALONICA" 11TH CENTURY 14TH-CENTURY FRAME

48. ICON "THE VIRGIN ENTHRONED". 12TH CENTURY

49, 50. ICON "ST JOHN THE FORERUNNER". 14TH CENTURY, FACE AND OBVERSE

51. "PHOTIUS" MOUNTING OF
ICON "THE VIRGIN OF VLADIMIR"
EARLY 15TH CENTURY. DETAIL

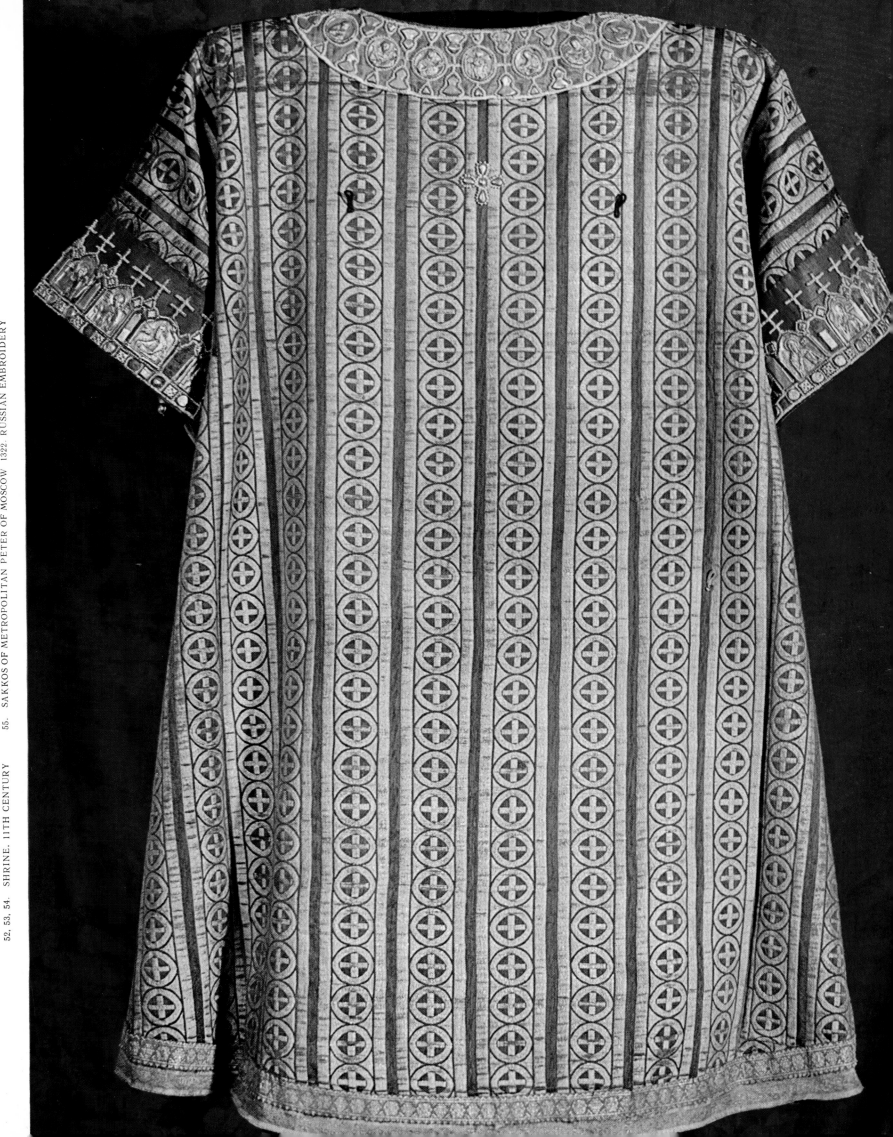

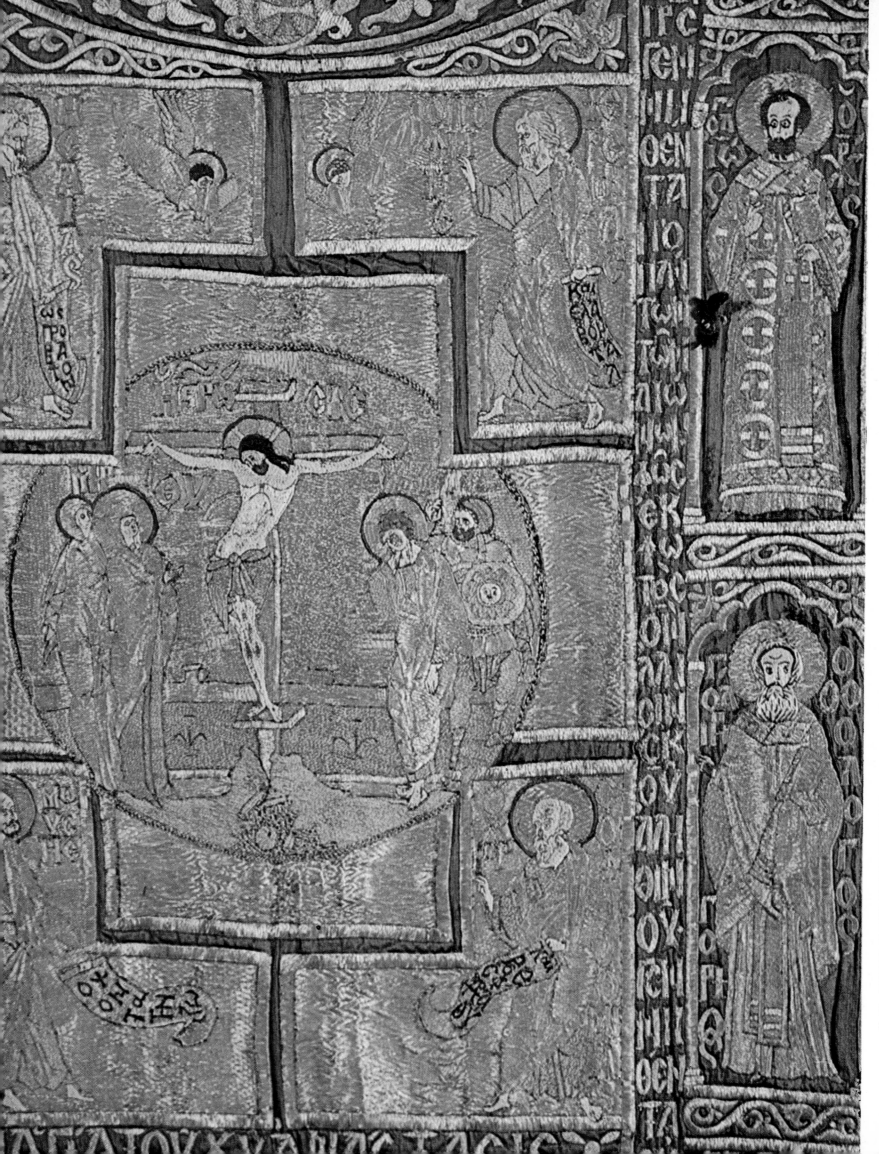

58, 59. "MINOR" SAKKOS OF METROPOLITAN PHOTIUS OF MOSCOW. MID-14TH CENTURY

RUSSIAN ART
OF THE
16th
CENTURY

T THE END of the fifteenth century a repository of state treasures, which subsequently became known as the Armoury, was established. The size of the Grand Prince's coffers had even by that time reached such dimensions that a special stone building, later known as the Treasury, was built in 1484, and to it were transferred the valuables stored in the vaults of the Kremlin churches and cathedrals. The Treasury of the Grand Prince, which at the beginning was no more than his personal possessions, began to acquire the features of a state repository during the period of the emergence of the centralized Russian state.

In 1504, on the instructions of the Grand Prince Ivan III of Moscow (1462—1505), the first inventory of the sealed chests containing the treasures of the Prince was taken. In 1511, during the reign of Vassili III, the post of Court Armourer as guardian of the court treasures was instituted. The first Armourer was A. M. Saltykov, who held this office from 1511 to 1522. Sixteenth century records mention the Kremlin Treasury twice: the first time in 1547 on the occasion of the coronation of Ivan the Terrible (1530-84) and the second time in the same year in reference to "a great Moscow fire", when mention is made of the fact that "the treasury of the great tsar was burnt down, and the Armoury was burnt with all military weapons". Despite the devastation wrought by the fire, the Treasury of the Grand Prince of Moscow continued to grow during the sixteenth century and was added to by various items made by master craftsmen of weapons and jewellery.

After the establisment of diplomatic relations with countries of East and West, the Treasury began to receive ambassadorial gifts from envoys from Poland, Germany, England, Denmark and other countries, and these were stored in the Kremlin Treasury. At the same time many "overseas goods" were acquired by trade with "guests" (foreign merchants) and other foreigners. Ivan the Terrible showed a great interest in precious stones and speared no expense to buy them abroad and from European and Asian merchants visiting Russia. At the same time the sixteenth century Armoury was not merely a storehouse, but a workshop too. We know about the silversmiths and goldsmiths and other specialists working there from the gifts of Ivan the Terrible to the cathedrals of the Moscow Kremlin and various monasteries throughout the country. Russian master craftsmen produced table ware for the tsar's court in great quantities. The inventories of Ivan the Terrible for the years 1581 and 1582 refer, among other things, to "twenty gold dippers" and "twenty gold cups". The Russian Tsar never missed an opportunity to display the wealth of his possessions in the Armoury to foreign envoys, merchants and other guests of honour. The splendour of the Tsar's court during the reign of Ivan the Terrible was truly fantastic, according to foreign visitors. For example, the German Ambassador Kobenzel wrote in 1576: "He wore a royal mantle and a diadem.... which surpassed the crowns of the kings... of Spain, France or the Grand Duke of Tuscany, and even the crown of Caesar himself and the King of Hungary and Bohemia cannot be compared to it..." Kobenzel goes to say that "...the Moscow court has so much silver and gold that it is almost impossible to count all the vessels".

During the reign of Tsar Feodor Ivanovich between 1584 and 1598 the splendour of the court did not diminish. For example, the dress of Tsarina Irina, Tsar Feodor's wife, worn on the occasion of a reception for Jeremiah, the Ratriarch of Constantinople in 1589, left a deep impression of magnificence on all who were present. Nicholas Vorkoc, the Austrian Ambassador, was able to count up to 1,000 gold dishes in the Faceted Palace of the Kremlin. The court of Tsar Boris Godunov (1598—1605) in addition to splendour, showed a high degree of artistic taste. During his reign the custom of displaying court riches for the benefit of foreign visitors continued, and Don Juan of Persia wrote in a dispatch of 1599: "the riches of the Treasury are as difficult to imagine as they are to describe... The arsenal is so big and so richly equipped that it can easily arm 50,000 cavalry..." The Armoury still contains much cold steel, fire-arms and armour from the rich arsenal of Ivan the Terrible, including lances, spears, pikes, halberts, helmets, chain mail.

The splendid specimens of Russian armour are of great interest. Chain mail is the oldest kind of armour. Altogether there are 27 pieces of chain mail in the collection. Among them the most famous is the hauberk of Tsar Boris Godunov. Some of the hatchets, puncheons, picks, halberts and sabres bear inscriptions which refer to their owners, famous boyards of the sixteenth century, for example, the pick belonging to Feodor Andreevich Teliazhevsky and one belonging to Vassili Ivanovich Turenin-Obolensky. Cold steel was usually decorated with engraved designs and handles were usually covered with leather or velvet.

The Armoury has a great number of old standards. The most interesting among them are those made from 1552 to 1560, during Ivan the Terrible's time, and the standards of Yermak Timofeyevich of 1581-2. Some of them were made by the standard painters of the Armoury.

By the mid-sixteenth century the workshops in the Moscow Kremlin had evolved their own artistic style. The works of Russian applied art exhibited in the Armoury are not only on a par with the finest works of art from abroad, but even surpass some of them. Most of them were made to order for the tsar. The second biggest purchaser was the Church.

The technique of niello reached its summit for skill and expressiveness during the sixteenth century, and the work of this period has a characteristic rich black colouring, attaining an almost velvet-like quality, against a background of gold. Niello ornamentation and inscriptions were applied on gold objects in fine hatching, usually on smooth background. One of the most prominent masterpieces of the jeweller's art is the gold dish with chasing, presented by Ivan the Terrible to his bride the Caucasian Princess Maria Temryukovna, in 1561. The beautiful black niello design and the plaques with inscriptions around the rim are echoed in the chased spoons that go with the dish.

Besides luxury ware, icons in gold and silver mountings were to be found in the tsar's palace and the houses of the priests, boyards and nobility. The icon settings are the most valuable specimens of Russian decorative art. The chased ornamentation of the mountings and other gold and silver ware of the sixteenth century displays clear cut design, plasticity and almost three-dimensional effect. More often than not it incorporates a floral design with intertwined stems, flowers and leaves. The mid-sixteenth century saw the wide use of coloured enamels and in this technique the Russian masters achieved great skill. One example of the enamel technique of the period is the 1554 "mernaya" icon (such icons were made to the size of a new-born child in a royal family) of Tsarevich Ivan Ivanovich.

By the end of the sixteenth century the ornamentation of filigree and enamel-adorned luxury ware had become more intricate and elaborate. Flowers, leaves, rosettes and granulation work were included in the designs. A good example of this kind of work is the cover for the gospels made to order for Tsar Ivan the Terrible and donated to the Cathedral of Annunciation of the Moscow Kremlin in 1571. It is one of the best examples of decorative and applied art of the sixteenth century.

The sixteenth century saw great achievements not only in the production of arms and gold and silver ware, but also in Russian decorative and portrait embroidery. Since time immemorial embroidery has been one of the favourite arts of the Russian people. It was popular not only among women of the higher classes, but practically obligatory for every Russian woman.

All through the sixteenth and seventeenth centuries there were a number of workshops famous for embroidery, belonging to various princes and boyards: the Staritskys, Godunovs, Golitsyns and the famous Stroganov merchant family. Each one of these workshops evolved its own artistic features.

By the end of the sixteenth century the centre of embroidery had shifted to the Tsarina's Workshop, which produced exquisite examples of Russian needlework: lace and embroidery in coloured silk, gold and silver thread, pearls and precious stones, for both church and nobility. We regret to say that history has not preserved a single name either of the women who did this work or of the workers and jewellers of the Armoury. The Armoury collection contains a great number of items of sixteenth century portrait embroidery, mostly covers for the Holy Sacrament and a pall belonging to the so-called Godunov school. Practically all of them were made under the close supervision of Tsarina Irina Godunova herself. During this period a simpler technique of silk embroidery was replaced by gold and silver thread embroidery. The embroidery designs, like the chased ornamentation of metal ware of the period, were based on floral designs borrowed from folk art. The main features were clarity and rhythmic simplicity.

The decorative embroidery of the period can be best demonstrated by the orphreys on the sakkos worn by Metropolitan Anthony, the embroidered sakkos of Patriarch Nicon and the 1583 orphrey yoke for a sakkos.

Moscow's extensive trade connections were the channels through which "overseas textiles" reached Russia. Foreign materials were not only used to embroider upon, they were also the source of ornamental designs. The Moscow Kremlin was the centre of Russia's artistic life during the sixteenth century, especially the middle of the century. The finest Russian artists and craftsmen were to be found in Moscow. Many of the Russian works of art of the sixteenth century can be considered masterpieces of world art.

60. "BAIDANA" OF TSAR BORIS GODUNOV. 16TH CENTURY. DETAIL
61. "BAIDANA" OF TSAR BORIS GODUNOV. 16TH CENTURY ▶

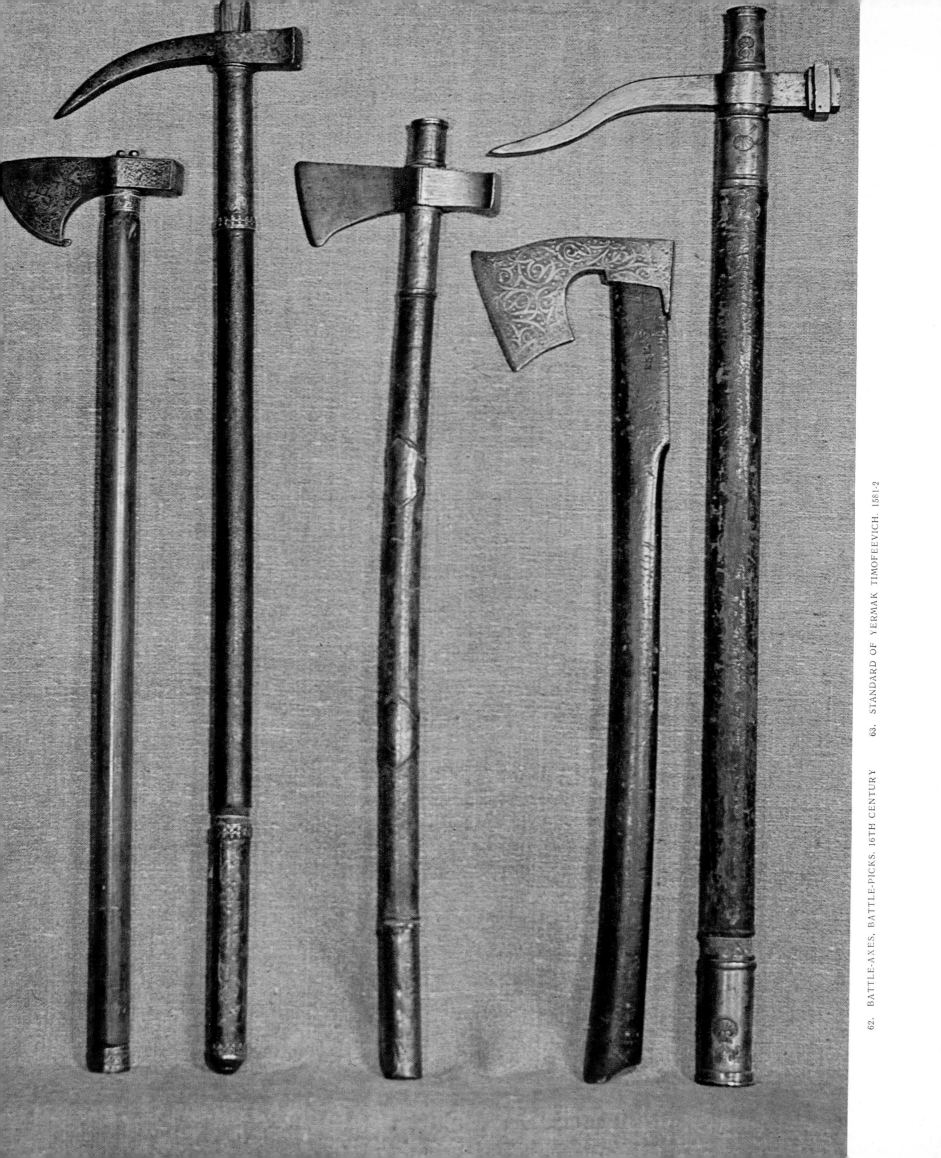

62. BATTLE-AXES, BATTLE-PICKS. 16TH CENTURY   63. STANDARD OF YERMAK TIMOFEEVICH. 1581-2

64. DISH OF TSARINA MARIA TEMRYUKOVNA. 1561

65. GOSPELS OF TSAR IVAN THE TERRIBLE. COVER. 1568 ▶

66. PANAGIA OF PATRIARCH JOB. 1589
SETTING. 12TH-CENTURY CAMEO. BYZANTIUM

67. CHANCEL CROSS. 1562

68. "MERNAYA" ICON "ST JOHN
CLIMACUS" IN MOUNTING. 1554

69. CENSER OF TSARINA IRINA. 1598

70. CHALICE OF TSARINA IRINA 1598 ▶

71. ICON "CHRIST ALMIGHTY" IN MOUNTING. SECOND HALF 16TH CENTURY

72. GOSPELS OF TSAR IVAN THE TERRIBLE. COVER. 1571 ▶

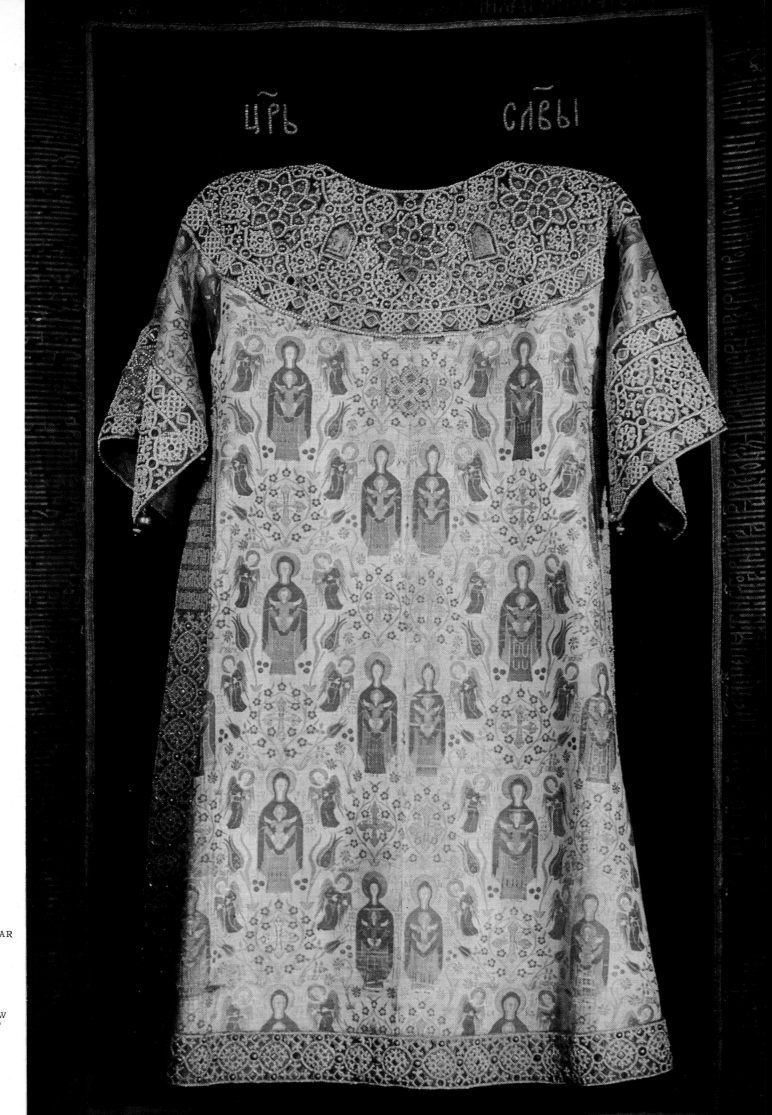

ЦРЬ СЛВЫ

73. SADDLE OF TSAR
BORIS GODUNOV
16TH CENTURY.
"POKROVETS".
17TH CENTURY

74 SAKKOS
OF METROPOLITAN
DIONYSIUS OF MOSCOW
LATE 16TH CENTURY

75. SAKKOS OF METROPOLITAN ANTHONY OF MOSCOW. SLEEVES. LATE 16TH CENTURY
76. PHELONION. EARLY 17TH CENTURY. TURKISH FABRIC ▶

77. CEREMENT. 1598   78. SAKKOS OF PATRIARCH NICON. 1654. LATE 16TH CENTURY RUSSIAN EMBROIDERY ▶

RUSSIAN ART
OF THE
17th
CENTURY

O F ALL THE ARMOURY collections that of seventeenth century art is most representative. It includes specimens made in the various workshops of the Moscow Kremlin: the Armoury, the Household and Coach-Making Shops, the Stables, the Tsarina's, the Gold and Silver Workshops.

The seventeenth century was the period when the activity of these workshops reached its zenith.

The most skilled master craftsmen gathered from all over the country worked here, and also foreign specialists. After the Polish and Swedish invaders were driven out of the country, Russia reached a new phase of historic development. The country's economic progress, its internal reorganisation and the broadening of its foreign contacts were all factors that speeded the process of forming a united Russian state. Seventeenth century art was the culmination of many centuries of old Russian traditions, and at the same time contained the seeds of the art of the new times. During the first quarter of the century the jewellers were given the task of restoring the splendour of the tsarist court, manufacturing new regalia, decorations, table ware for state occasions, mountings for icons and various church plate.

From the numerous and magnificent seventeenth century works of art still extant it is clear that during this period the Russian people were experiencing an upsurge of artistic and creative endeavour.

Russian armourers were renowned for their high degree of skill. They aimed at making their weapons light, durable, easy to handle, and beautiful. For quality, workmanship and artistic embellishment Russian weapons can stand comparison with the finest weapons made in East or West. The barrel-makers decorated the barrels with rich damascene ornamentation, and the stock-makers used bone, mother-of-pearl and various kinds of wood for inlaid decoration, or they covered the stock with ornamental carving.

The beauty of Russian harness and trappings has been known from earliest times. In the seventeenth century saddles, stirrups, bridles and horse cloths made in the Cavalry Workshop of the Kremlin were famous abroad. Rich elaborate designs and bright colours, skilfully distributed over the entire surface of the objects, emphasize the basic lines of the saddles, bridles and caparisons. Russian saddles were not only artistic and magnificently decorated, but were comfortable and light. They were of logical design, well suited to their purpose; with a high slightly forward-inclining pommel and a lower cantle the rider could turn easily in the saddle.

The Armoury has a considerable collection of Russian horse cloths, extremely interesting in design and decorative detail. However ornate the horse trappings were, the craftsmen always tried to keep within certain limits so that everything they produced was practical as well as decorative.

Russian embroiderers mastered to a high degree the most difficult and complex techniques involved in producing works of art; they knew the artistic possibilities of the materials they worked upon and were at home with the immense riches of ornamental composition.

Among the most famous workshops in the sixteenth-seventeenth centuries were those belonging to the royal and boyard families: the Staritskys, Godunovs and Golitsyns, and the famous Stroganov merchant family. However, the best was the Workshop of the Tsarina, housed in the women's quarters of the Terem Palace, immediately beneath the Tsarina's own chambers. Embroidery was usually done to the designs of the artists. Any text which might be incorporated was first put in by special artists. However, the embroiderers had not only to follow the design, but to choose the combinations of shades to bring out the essence of the drawing. The silk stitches used to fasten down the gold thread also formed geometric designs in addition to those of the basic embroidery and their infinite variety bears witness to the rich imagination of the embroiderers.

Russian embroidery was justly termed "needle painting". The Armoury collection contains some splendid works of art executed in decorative and portrait embroidery techniques dating back to the seventeenth century. Among the portrait embroidery are numerous palls, covers for Holy Sacraments, shrouds and icons, which were made not only in the Tsarina's Workshop but in other artistic centres of the country.

When an embroiderer used geometric or floral designs the embroidery was known as "floral" and later on as "ornamental" or "decorative". Splendid examples of this kind of work are the collar, hem and cuffs of many sakkoses and phelonions, epitrachelions, separate sleeves, mitres and many other items. The various designs of decorative embroidery which incorporate intertwined stems and grasses have much in common with the chased and carved designs on metal work and traditional embroidery. Seventeenth century embroidery designs were predominantly floral and there were endless variations. Besides the stylized floral designs there were quite realistic natural-looking flowers and leaves. A favourite pattern was the continuously twinning stem and another resembling metal lattice work with sharp, rounded or other figured edges. Oriental designs are frequently seen in Russian embroidery—hyacinths, tulips and pomegranate motifs. In keeping with the general tradition of Russian art the embroiderers used to pad their needlework, which meant added relief and an interesting play of light and shade. Precious stones started playing a more important role, with pearls being given a prominent place in decorative embroidery. While adding richness, they at the same time softened the brilliance and vividness of the cloth and gold embroidery. Russian embroiderers achieved magnificence and a high degree of beauty by the careful grading of pearls and the clever use of gems. The Silver and Gold Halls of the Moscow Kremlin constituted the main artistic centre of the country during the seventeenth century. The skill of Russian master craftsmen rose to a peak point in artistic treatment of metals: casting, beating, incising, chasing, enamelling and niello work. At the beginning of the seventeenth century decoration on gold and silver ware followed the economical ornamentation popular in the sixteenth century, the most usual patterns being stylized floral and grass designs and the favourite colour range soft pastels with light blue predominating. Sapphire was the most frequently used gems. Then little by little the designs changed. The palaces of the nobility which were painted in bright colours and in which coloured tiling was used for interiors and exteriors demanded a greater magnificence of decorative detail. Designs become more involved and increasingly ornate. Beside the floral motifs there appear human figures and animals and motifs derived from popular folk prints and etchings. From the second half of the seventeenth century ornamentation becomes richer, more elaborate and picturesque.

For instance, to give an additional almost three-dimensional effect to a niello inlay light hatching along the outlines was used. Many objects bear additional inscriptions, either incised or done in niello or black enamel.

There was also abundant use of precious stones. In addition to sapphires, topazes and rubies, wide use was made of diamonds and emeralds, and frequently, gold and silver ware were set with entire plaques studded with precious stones. Stones of round or irregular form, flat-cut gems were also used in low "nest" settings. More attention was now paid to the purity of the stone and the intensity of its colour. Towards the end of the seventeenth century there appeared group compositions on biblical subjects, allegorical representations of the seasons of the year and subjects derived from folk epics and fairy tales. Chasing and enamelling were the two most popular techniques. A striving for heightened decorativeness, involved detailing and ornateness led in certain cases to overburdening with precious stones, pearls and enamels. Enamels became so bright and intense that their brilliance rivalled that of precious stones. Beside the exquisite enamelling on gold and silver, enamels with filigree ornamentation became widely popular. Here white and green predominated and the design included a great number of white dots in imitation of the traditional pearl outlining in embroidery. Moscow jewellers used enamel not only on flat surfaces, but on chased and almost sculptured objects too. The chasing technique reached a high degree of sophistication at that time; the popular chased pattern of flowers and buds on long curved stems with rich foliage at times covered the entire surface of an object and frequently, the pattern was reinforced with granulation work.

The character of carved decoration also underwent a marked change. The fine hatching which followed the outlines of the design softened every line, and there was a resemblance to the techniques used in brushwork.

Towards the end of the seventeenth century a number of objects were executed in purely pictorial engraving technique on subjects taken from book illustrations and etchings. They were usually framed by floral or spiral patterns.

Working as they did side by side with foreign masters, and getting to know the wares brought from West and East, the Russian master craftsmen enlarged the subject matter of their ornamental designs. While assimilating oriental and western motifs, they evolved a Russian traditional design.

During the last quarter of the seventeenth century the Gold and Silver Workshops in the Kremlin started producing luxury ware with austere lines and smooth surfaces, without adornment except for separate spots of colour in the form of precious stones and plaques with enamel patterns. The achievements of Russian seventeenth century art were a logical link in the further development of Russian art.

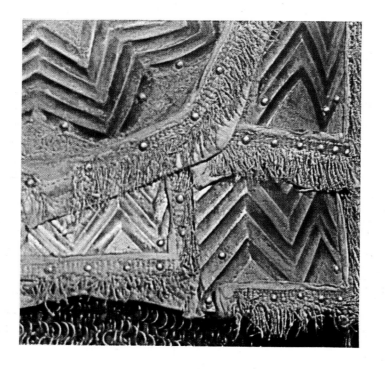

79. "ZERTSALOS". MADE BY NIKITA DAVYDOV. 1663. DETAIL
80. "ZERTSALOS". MADE BY NIKITA DAVYDOV. 1663 ▶

81. "BAKHTERETS" OF TSAR MIKHAIL FEODOROVICH. MADE BY KONON MIKHAILOV. 1620

82. SADDLE OF TSAR MIKHAIL FEODOROVICH. MADE BY IVAN POPOV AND COMPANIONS. 1637-8. "CHALDAR" OF TSAR ALEXEI MIKHAILOVICH. SECOND HALF 17TH CENTURY

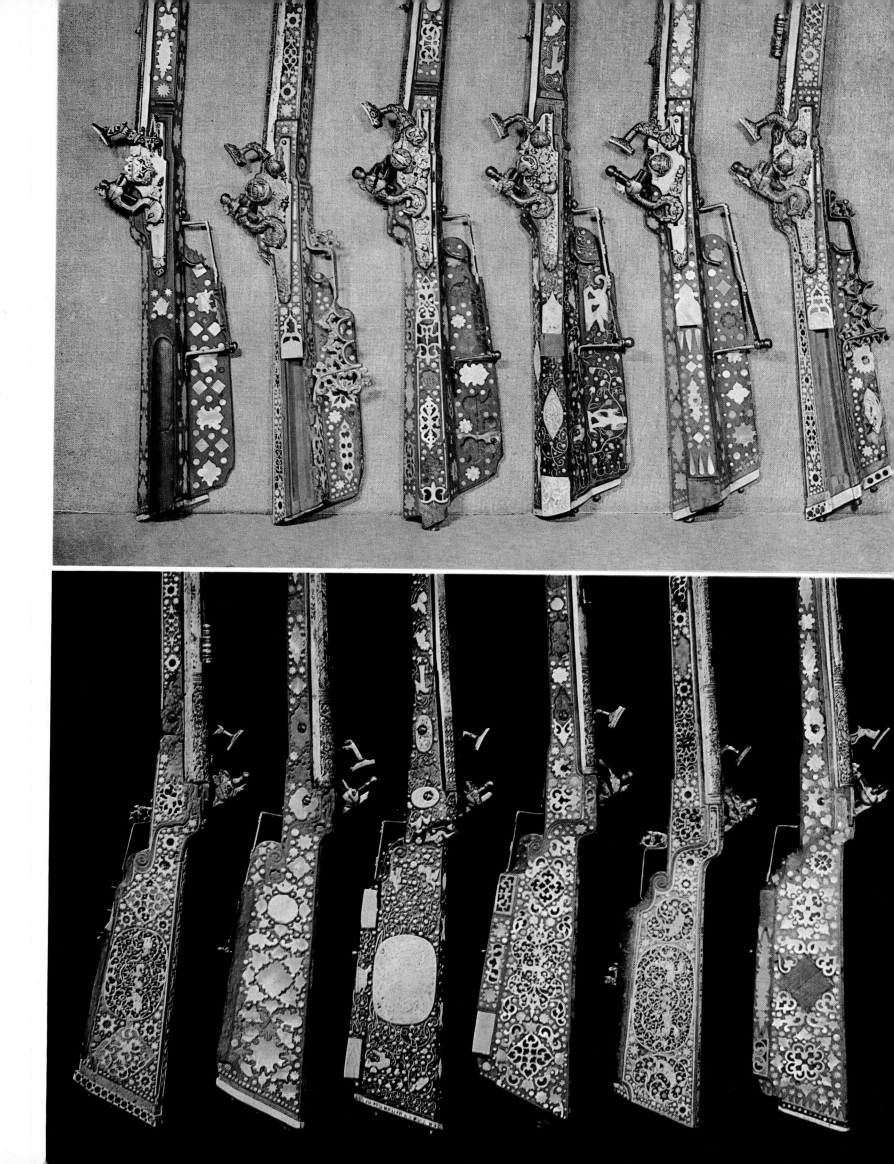

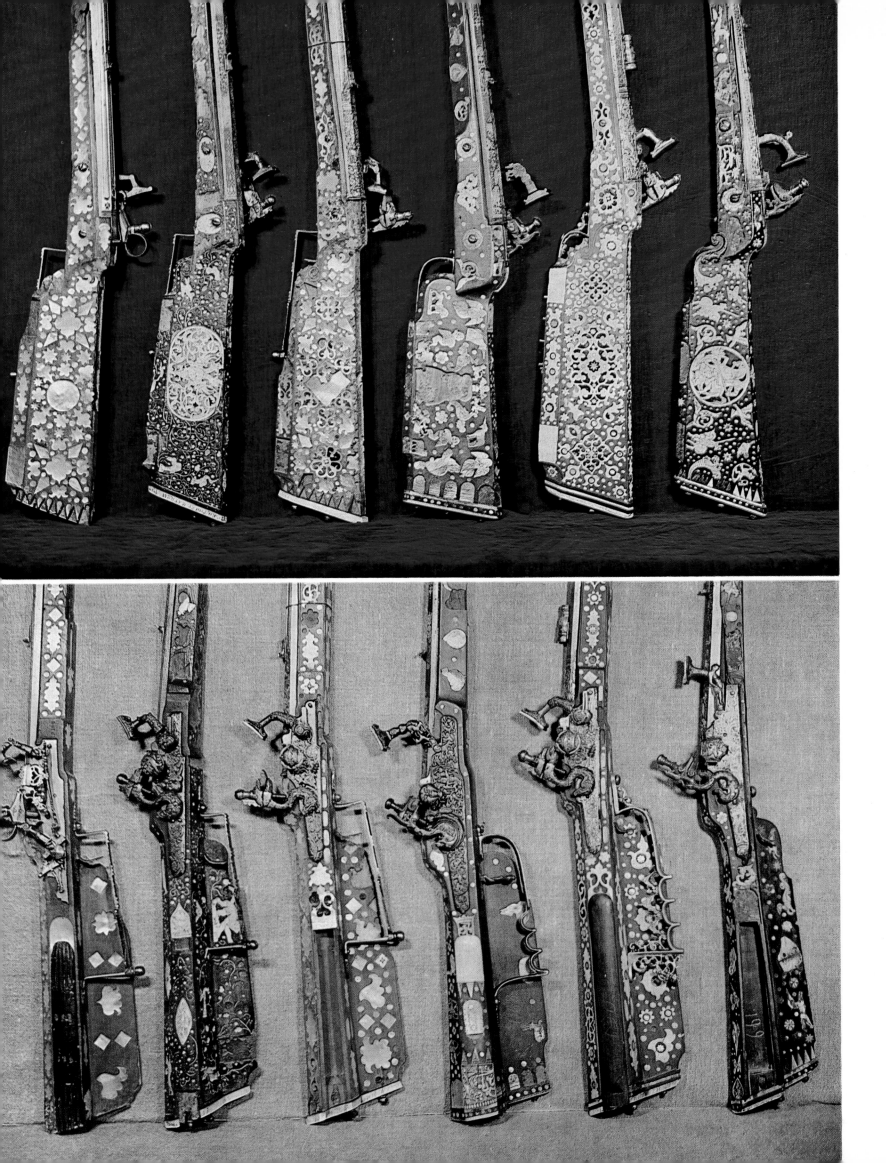

83, 84, 85, 86. ARQUEBUSES. MATCHLOCKS. BUTT-STOCKS. 17TH CENTURY
87. "PRAPOR" OF VLADIMIR REGIMENTS OF RUSSIAN ARMY. 17TH CENTURY

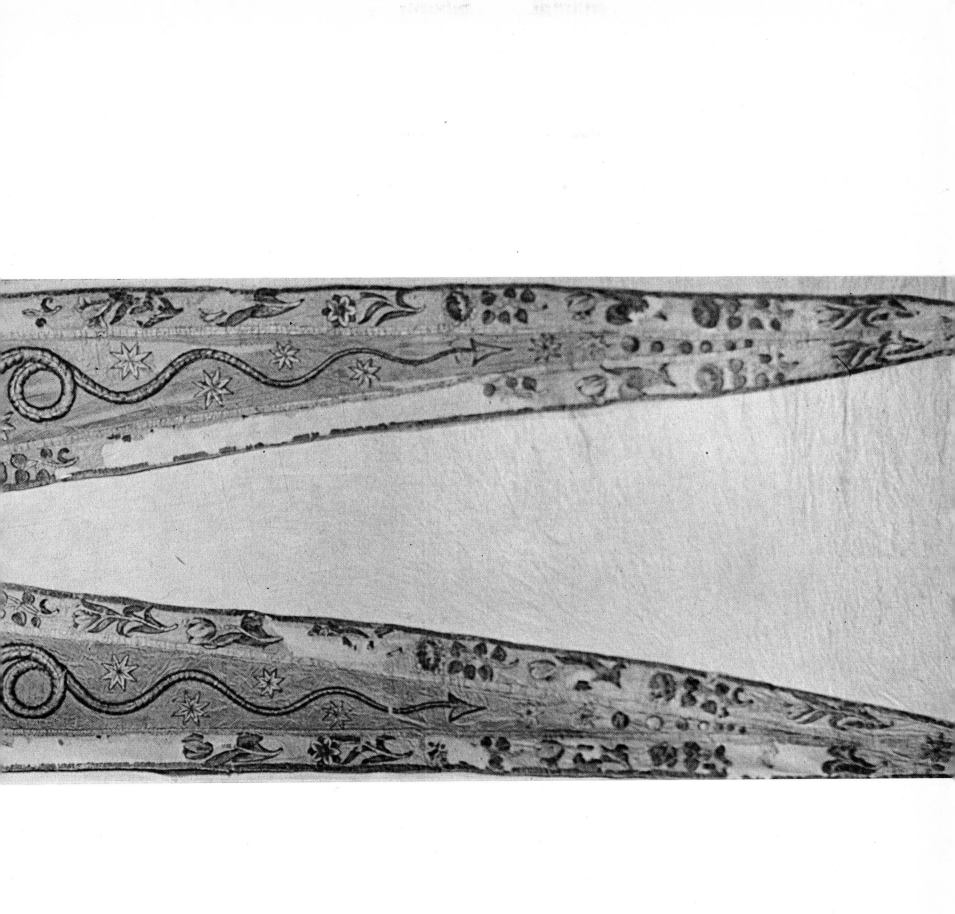

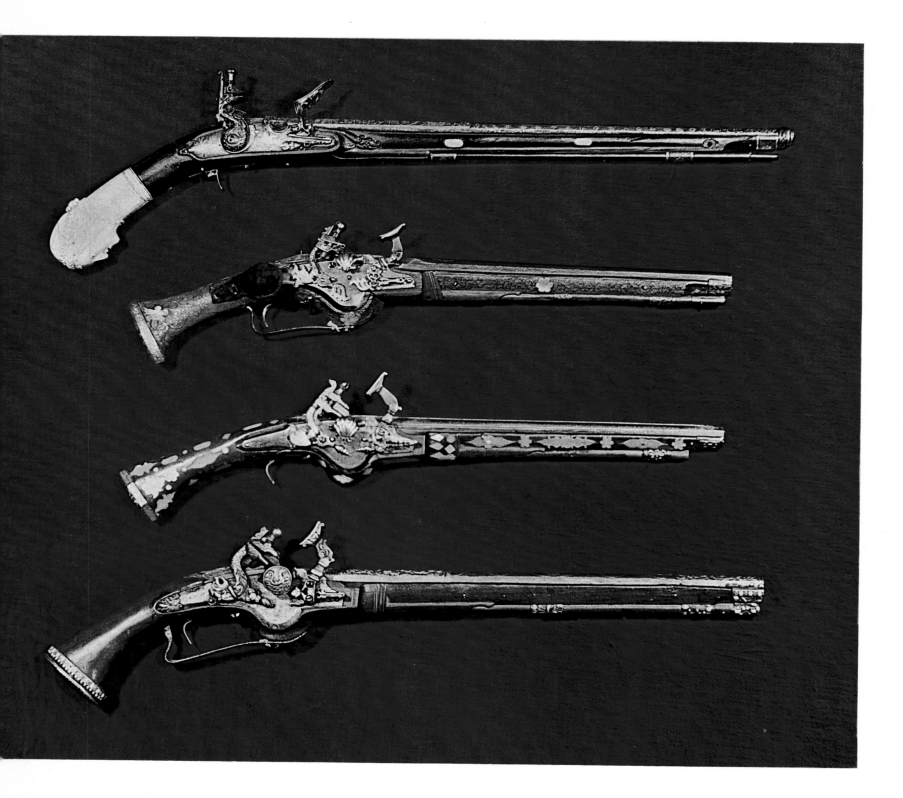

88. PISTOLS. 17TH CENTURY

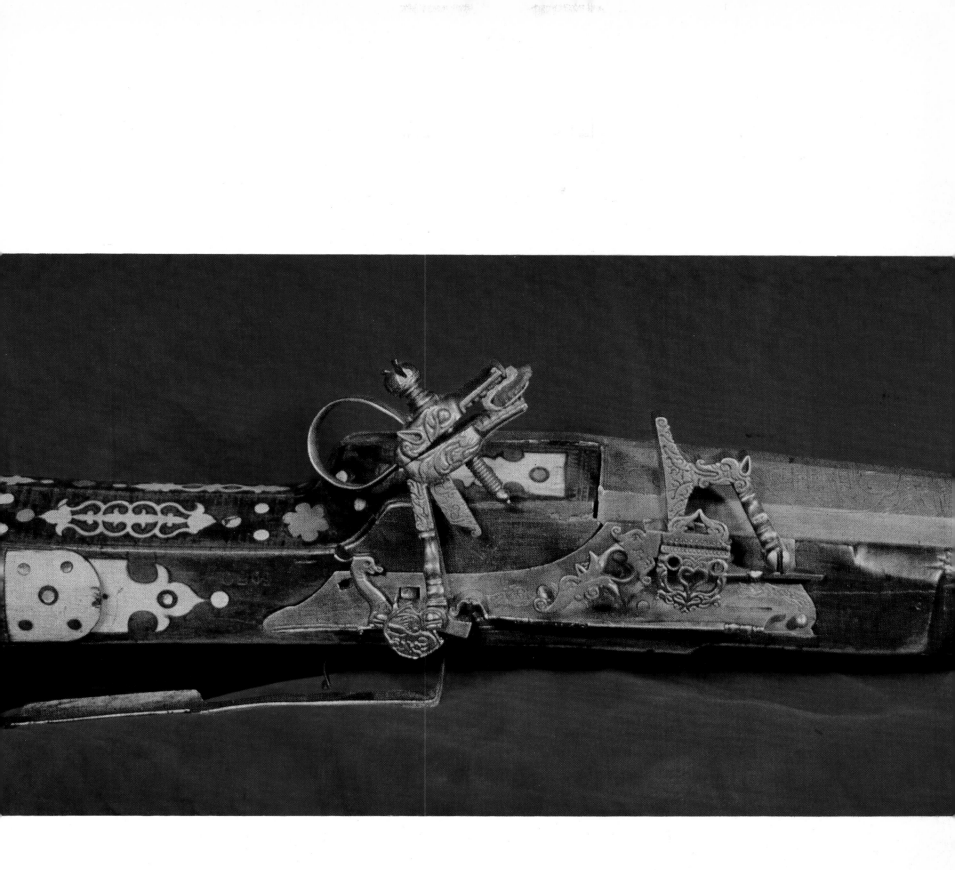

89. GUN-"TYUFIAK" OF TSAR ALEXEI MIKHAILOVICH. MATCHLOCK. MADE BY GRIGORI VIATKIN

90. GUNNER "ALAM". 17TH CENTURY

91. GUNNER "ALAM". 17TH CENTURY

94. "SAADAK" FROM GRAND ROBES OF STATE OF TSAR MIKHAIL FEODOROVICH. 1628.
COAT OF ARM OF THE CITY OF MOSCOW. DETAIL

95. "SAADAK" FROM THE GRAND ROBES OF STATE OF TSAR MIKHAIL FEODOROVICH.
CASE FOR BOW QUIVER FOR ARROWS. 1628 ▶

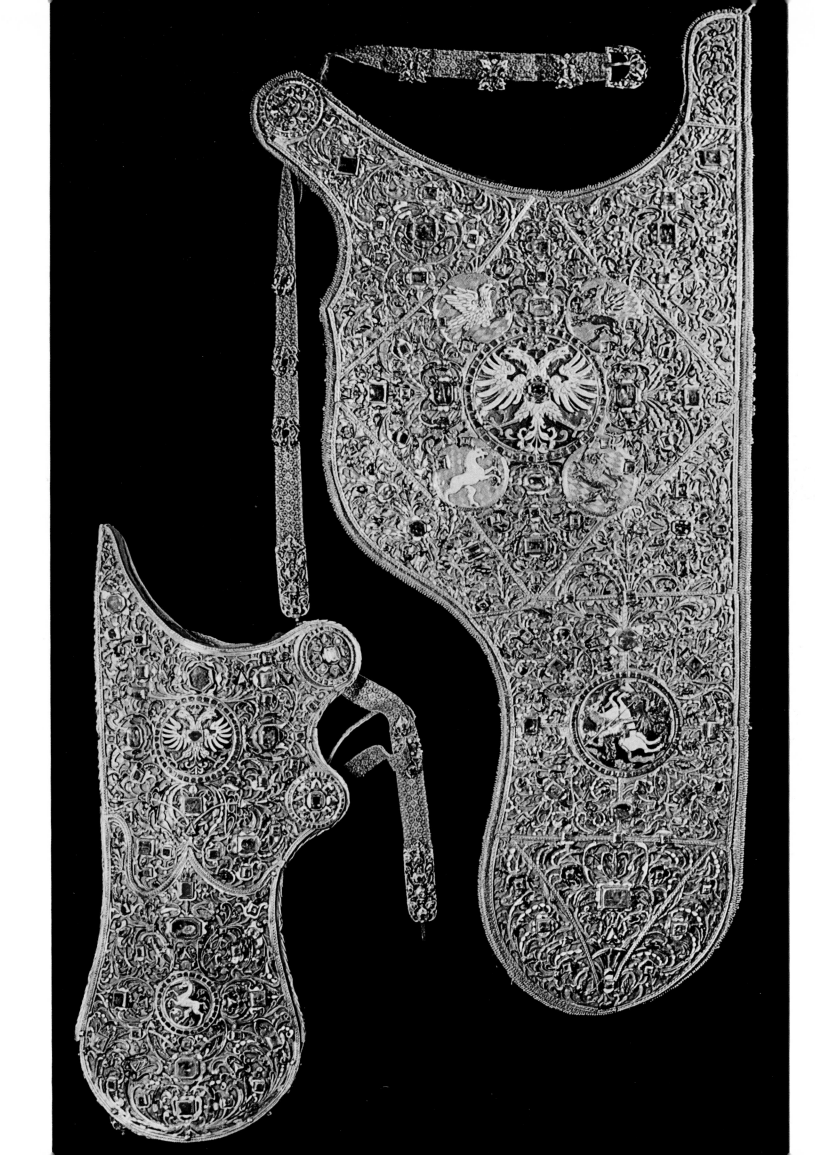

96. GRAND ROBES OF STATE OF TSAR MIKHAIL FEODOROVICH
CAP OF STATE. SCEPTRE. ORB. 1627-8

97. DIAMOND CAP OF STATE OF TSAR PETER THE GREAT. 1682-9 ▶

98. HOLSTER. 17TH CENTURY

99. DETAILS OF CEREMONIAL TSAR HORSE'S TRAPPINGS. 17TH CENTURY

◄ 100. "BRATINA" OF DYAK MIKHAIL DANILOV.
FIRST THIRD 17TH CENTURY

◄ 101. DIPPER OF TSAR MIKHAIL FEODOROVICH
FIRST HALF 17TH CENTURY

102. DIPPER OF TSAR MIKHAIL FEODOROVICH
MADE BY TRETYAK PESTRIKOV AND SON. 1624

103. FUNERAL "BRATINA" OF TSAR MIKHAIL
FEODOROVICH. FIRST HALF 17TH CENTURY

104　TRIPTYCH WITH THE ICON "THE VIRGIN ELEUSA" OF DUMA DYAK IVAN GRIAZEV. FIRST THIRD 17TH CENTURY

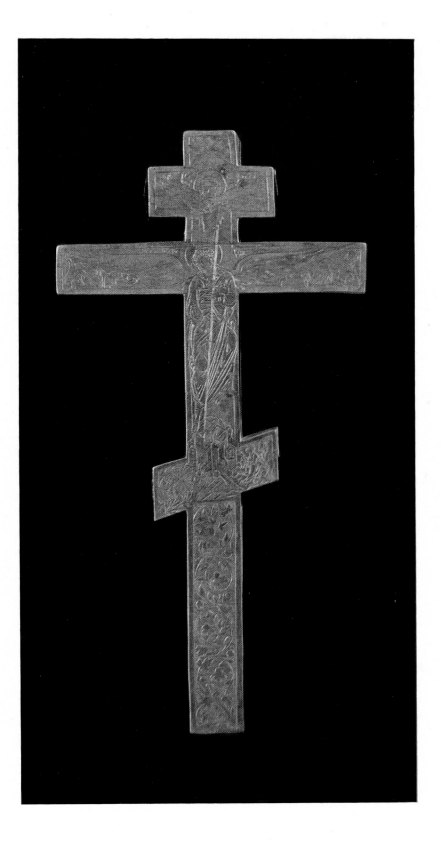

105. CROSS. 1636. REVERSE SIDE

106. "ENDOVA" OF BOYARD VASSILI STRESHNEV. 1644

107. GLASS. SECOND HALF 17TH CENTURY

108. "TAREL". 1664

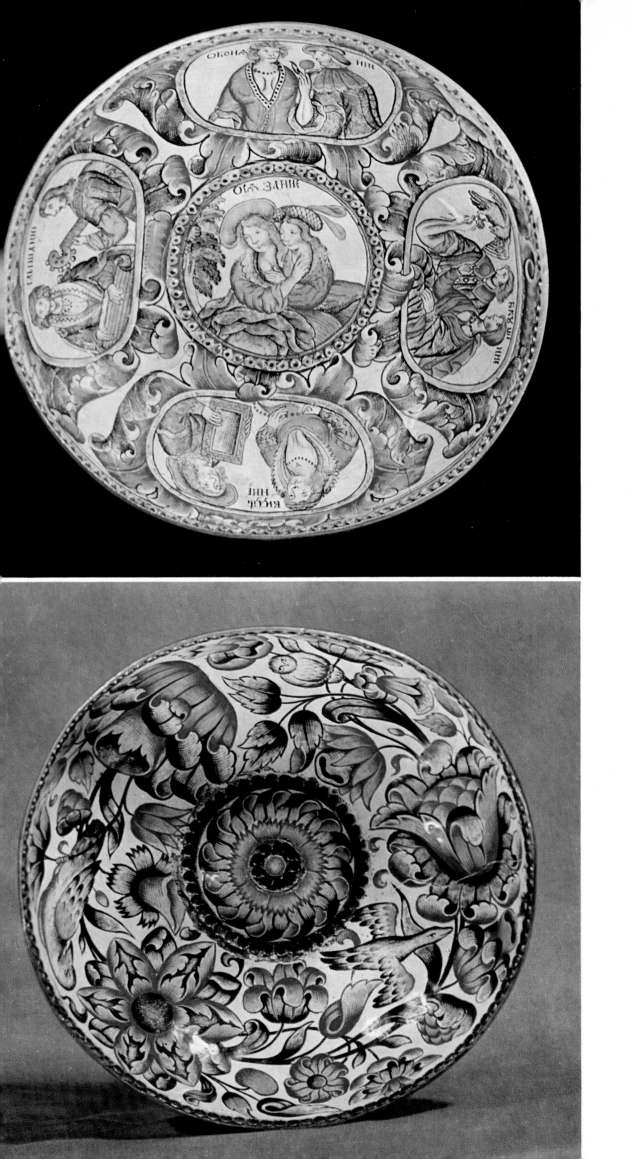

109, 110, 111, 112. BOWLS AND PLATES
LAST THIRD 17TH CENTURY

113. PANAGIA OF PATRIARCH JOASAPH II.
SETTING MADE BY MIKHAIL YAKOVLEV 1671.
12TH-CENTURY CAMEO. BYZANTIUM

114. BOWL OF TSAR ALEXEI MIKHAILOVICH. 1653

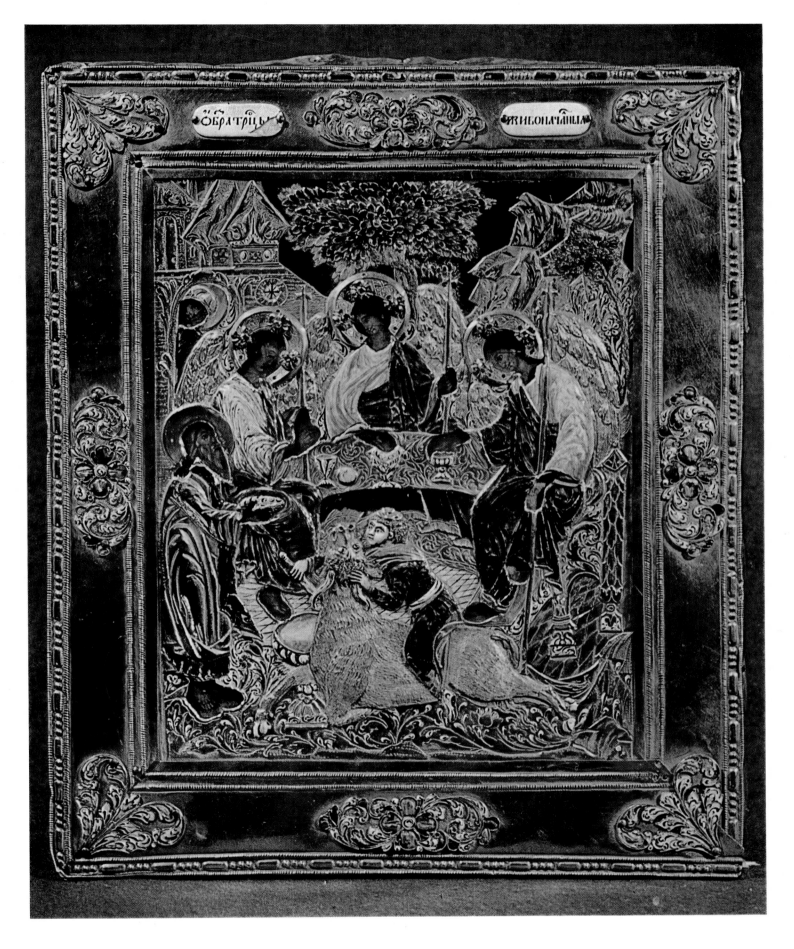

115. ICON "THE TRINITY" IN MOUNTING. 1676-82

116. SAKKOS OF PATRIARCH PITIRIM. SECOND HALF 17TH CENTURY. ITALIAN FABRIC   117. THE GOSPELS COVER 1678

И оучени...
стъртир...
часѣ, ...
слава, ...
ІнсУже...
длеемъ...
дни н...
леви ѿ...
ша во...
гдѣ е̑ст...
їѹдейск...
ѕвѣздѫ...
и прїидо...
е̑мѹ...
царь с...

М...

здѣ набл...
а́нна крт...
бы́сть цар...
дни и́злво...
повелѣ да...
оусѣкнѹ і...
цѣ и при...
на блюдѣ...
и ѿнесе ма...
стѹпльше...
взѧша т...
бо́ша е̑...
сти́ша ін...
інсъ ѿн...
бли въпѹст...

АЙ ДАСѢѢ
НУ ОБА ПА
Н ПРІНДО
ОЗОБАША
ДОША НА
ДѪЖЕ НЕН
Н МНѠГН
ША, ЗАНЕ НЕ
НЫ ЗЕМЛН
КВШУ ПРИ-
НЕ НЕ НМѢ
НСХОША
ША ВТЕРНІ
НПОДАВНН

ГД

СОБРАВ
Н Н
А ВО
ГДѢ
ОНН
НДАЛЕѢ
ТАКѠ
ОКОМЪ
МЛѢ ІУ
МЕНШН
ДОВЫ
ВОЖДЬ
Н МОА
ДЪ ТАН
НІСПЫ

МИ, Е.

122. ICON "THE VIRGIN
OF VLADIMIR" 17TH CENTURY

123. PALL FOR SEPULCHRE OF
METROPOLITAN JONAH
OF MOSCOW. 1657

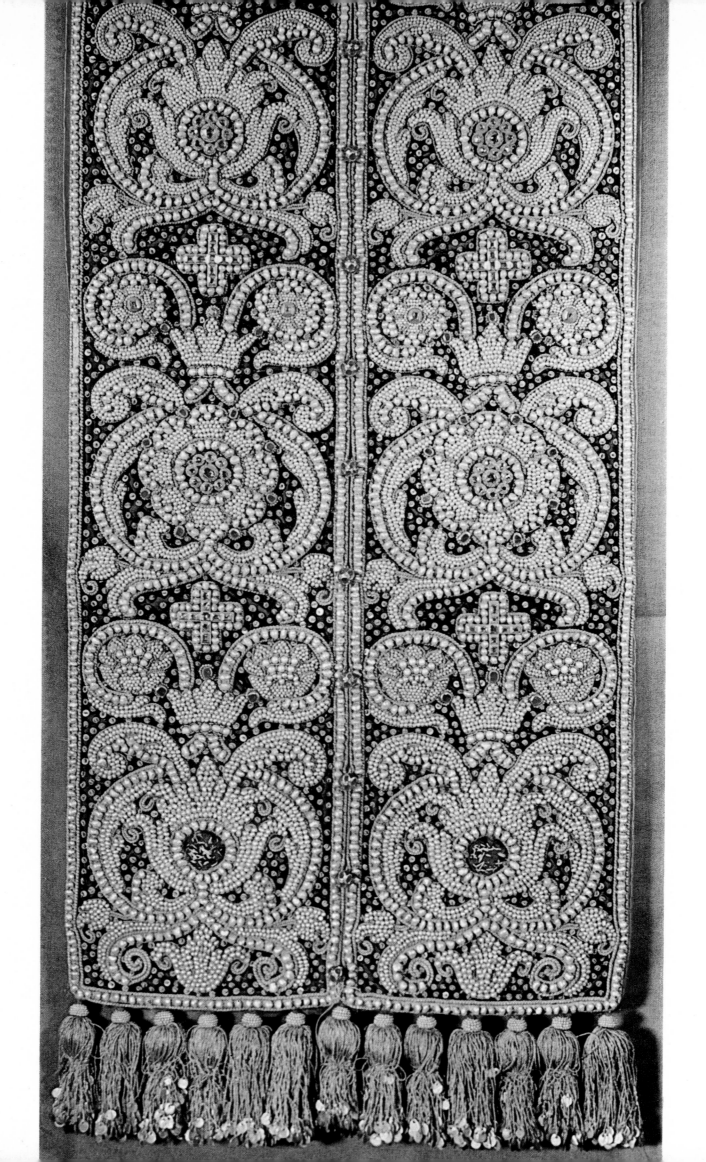

124. STOLE. 17TH CENTURY. DETAIL   125. PHELONION. 17TH CENTURY. DETAIL. ITALIAN FABRIC

126　INFANT COACHES OF TSAR PETER THE GREAT. SECOND HALF 17TH CENTURY
127　"PLATNO" OF TSAR PETER THE GREAT. 17TH CENTURY ▶

PERSIAN and TURKISH ART

OF THE

13-17 th

CENTURIES

PERSIAN AND TURKISH applied art forms an interesting part of the large and diverse collection of masterpieces in the Armoury. They are represented in the main by 16th and 18th century works. The Cap of Monomachos is the only exhibit of an earlier period. It dates back to the late 13th—early 14th century, but the question of its place of origin has not yet been settled. The majority of Russian and Soviet researchers consider it is from the Orient, but some believe it to be the work of a Byzantine master.

The collection consists primarily of works brought to Moscow by Persian and Turkish envoys, merchants and representatives of Constantinople ecclesiasts as gifts to the Russian tsars and Patriarchs.

Russia's trade ties with Persia and Turkey were formed towards the end of the fifteenth century. For the first time Russian envoys, from Prince Ivan III of Moscow (1462-1505), arrived in Constantinople in 1495 to arrange unhampered trade for Russian merchants in Turkey. Diplomatic and trade relations between Persia and Russia were established in the 16th century but back in the fifteenth century Persian merchants were bringing their wares to Amztarakani (present-day Astrakhan) and in the 16th-17th century trade with these countries acquired a regular and intensive character and played a leading role in the general foreign trade of Russia. Russia exported to the countries of the Orient iron, copper, firearms, helmets, armour, silverware, furs, leather, linen, sugar, honey and other merchandise. Special presents sent to Oriental potentates at times included live wild animals. In their turn Persian merchants brought to Moscow and other Russian towns "silks of various colours and texture, Kyzyl-Bash velvet, brocade, taffeta, valuable Persian carpets, Persian belts woven with gold thread, gold- and silver-embroidered linen, various cloth covers oversewn with pearls, expensive cups, ewers and other vessels, various rings with precious stones, saddles and horse trappings, sabres . . . "

In keeping with diplomatic etiquette the presenting of gifts was obligatory for envoys. After gifts had been presented to the tsar every object was valued and passed on for safe keeping in Treasury, to be removed only with the express permission of the tsar.

In appraising presents only the value of the metal, textiles and precious stones were taken into consideration and their artistic qualities and the degree of skill put into them were estimated only in rare cases.

From 16th-17th century records still in existence we can identify a whole number of objects, determine the name of the giver and the date of presentation. According to such historical documents we know that Lachin-Bek, the envoy of Shah Abbas I (1587-1629) brought a unique golden throne in 1604 as a gift to Tsar Boris Godunov. The shape of the throne and the character of the decorations are typical of the sixteenth century Persian art. The throne is entirely covered with a sheet of gold, with an overall fine floral pattern, and is studded with dark-red rubies, individual pearls and turquoises of various shades.

One of the most sumptuous presents of the sixteenth century was the "diamond" throne presented by an Armenian trading company in Persia in 1659 to Tsar Alexei Romanov in appreciation of the right of tax-free trade with Russia.

Horse trappings were the most common gifts from Persia—lavishly decorated saddles, stirrups, caparisons and bridles. In the countries of the Orient the horse was considered the closest friend of man and its trappings were accordingly magnificently decorated. The majority of the saddles and bridles on view in the Armoury are decorated with jasper and mother-of-pearl plaques studded with rubies, emeralds and pearls. Saddles are covered with velvet and brocade and decorated with silver or gold inlay designs. All documents between 1689 and 1692 mention that the favourite stone used in the decoration of horse trappings was turquoise, which was held in especial esteem in Persia and was supposed to have miraculous qualities. Persian horse cloths give a good idea of the pattern and colouring of Persian fabrics. There is a refined choice of hues: pink, light and dark blue, green and brown. The fine floral and geometrical ornament is fluid, light and beautiful. The pattern often incorporated birds, animals and human figures. Old inventories describe fabrics with designs of "people and animals, fishes and trees, and golden birds". The inventory of the personal belongings of Ivan the Terrible included "Kyzyl-Bash brocade of pink on cherry-red with patterns of human figures, young and old, and birds." Tsar Feodor Ivanovich was presented with "Kyzyl-Bash brocade of black and white silk, with a pattern of men on horseback and leopards pouncing on goats . . . "

The most popular of the floral motifs incorporate tulips, irises, hyacinths and carnations on long curved stems. Persian fabrics were well known throughout the world. Brocades, silks, velvets and particularly Kashan velvets were famous for their delicate design and exquisite colouring. The 16th century horse cloth and caftan are excellent examples of Persian fabrics of the time.

One of the most outstanding masterpieces of the 16th century Persian art is the Damascus steel shield made by the master craftsman Mumin-Muhammed, which belonged to the well known Russian army leader Boyard F. M. Mstislavsky. The shield is forged from a single sheet of the best steel. Its surface is encrusted with gold. The technique of steel-hammering to achieve a very hard and at the same time flexible Damascus steel of beautiful design was know to the mastev craftsmen in India and Persia, and to a certain degree in Azerbaijan. This masterpiece is unequalled for its fine workmanship. The gold damascene work on the steel is lavish and of unusually artistic workmanship.

Persian goldsmiths were familiar with many techniques of work on metal: chasing, engraving, *repoussé*, enamelling and niello. All Persian ware is striking in colouring and richly decorated. Artistically embellished maces, falchions and so on were in great demand in Russia. Their beauty of workmanship was in keeping with the rich apparel of the Russian boyards of the 17th century and an adornment to it. No less in demand in Russia were works by Turkish masters. Russia exported to Turkey agricultural produce, handicraft work such as cups, goblets, armour, helmets, fire-arms, and furs. It imported gold and crystal ware, semi-precious stones, carpets, and arms for ceremonial occasions. Seventeenth century Turkish artists went in for bright colours, large patterns, rich materials and somewhat heavy ornamentation. The ban imposed by the Sunnite faith on representations of living beings resulted in an unusual diversity of ornamental motifs. Unique precious textiles and rich horse trappings were the most important items of import in seventeenth century Russia. No other museum in the world has so complete and beautiful a collection of Turkish horse trappings as the Moscow Armoury.

Turkish saddles reflect to a certain degree the features of national style. They are covered in bright materials with large patterns and have gold and silver plaques studded with emeralds, rubies and big pearls on the side flaps, pommels and cantles. Many saddles are in addition embellished with chased metal plaques with turquoise, jasper carvings, and flowers worked in pearls.

The horse cloths of the collection are interesting not only as horse trappings in general, but as examples of rare textiles. Seventeen century Persian fabrics are well represented in the Armoury collection. In the main they go back to the first half of the century, when the Osman Empire was still a powerful state. This was a time when the Turkish craftsmen belonged in guilds which strictly controlled the production and character of the materials manufactured. The rules of the guilds frequently listed the kind of textiles to be produced, what colour and type of thread should be used and the width and the length of a bolt of cloth. Floral designs are the most predominant among the patterns. Tulips, carnations and wild roses framed in the typical "oval" with a pinched end were popular in all branches of Turkish art. Another favourite design was made up of stylized pomegranates and hyacinths. Other frequent designs were "fans": full blown carnations resembling fans, and "suns": medallions with twelve-point stars within them. These designs can be found in houses and mosques and on table ware. Another characteristic feature of Turkish textiles was sharply contrasting colours which heightened the decorative effect of the material. Red predominated, in combination with light and dark blues and green.

Turkish materials found their way into Russia through two channels: they were brought either for sale by oriental merchants or as gifts by the numerous Turkish envoys who visited Moscow yearly during the seventeenth century.

The masterpieces of Turkish ceremonial weapons and weapons of attack and defense: sabres, daggers, maces and quivers for holding bows and arrows were distinguished for their excellent material, workmanship and rich ornamentation, and some specimens are world famous. The most famous is the quiver presented to Tsar Alexei Mikhailovich in 1656, which is completely covered with chased gold and decorated with emeralds, rubies and diamonds. The inscription tells that it was made in Constantinople as a gift for the Russian tsar. Sheaths and hilts of Turkish swords and daggers were lavishly decorated.

The collection of Persian and Turkish masterpieces at the Armoury provides a wealth of material for a study of the applied art of these countries and at the same time is evidence of the broad ties of long standing between Russia and its neighbours, the countries of Asia Minor.

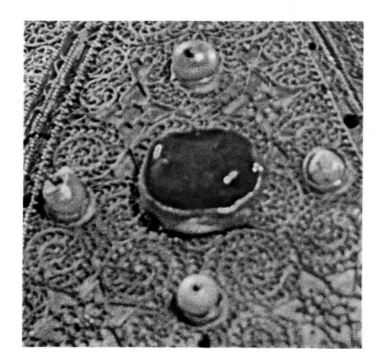

128. MONOMACHOS CAP OF STATE. LATE 13TH—EARLY
14TH CENTURY. DETAIL. ORIENT

129. MONOMACHOS CAP OF STATE. LATE 13TH—EARLY
14TH CENTURY. ORIENT ▶

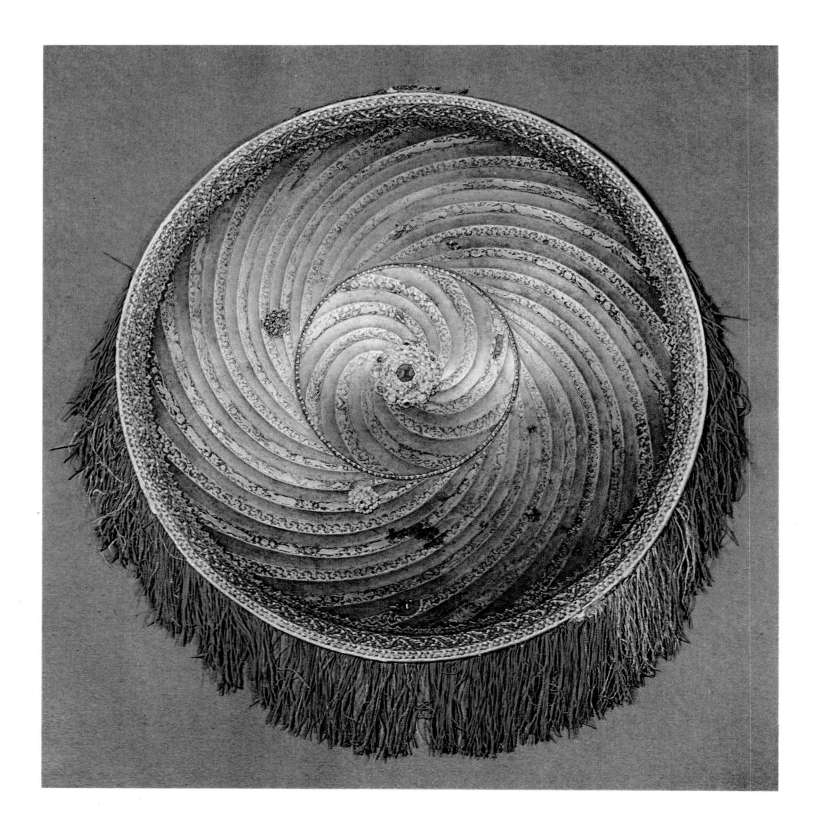

130. DAMASK STEEL SHIELD OF BOYARD FEODOR MSTISLAVSKY. MADE BY MUMIN-MOHAMMED. 16TH CENTURY. IRANIAN AZERBAIJAN

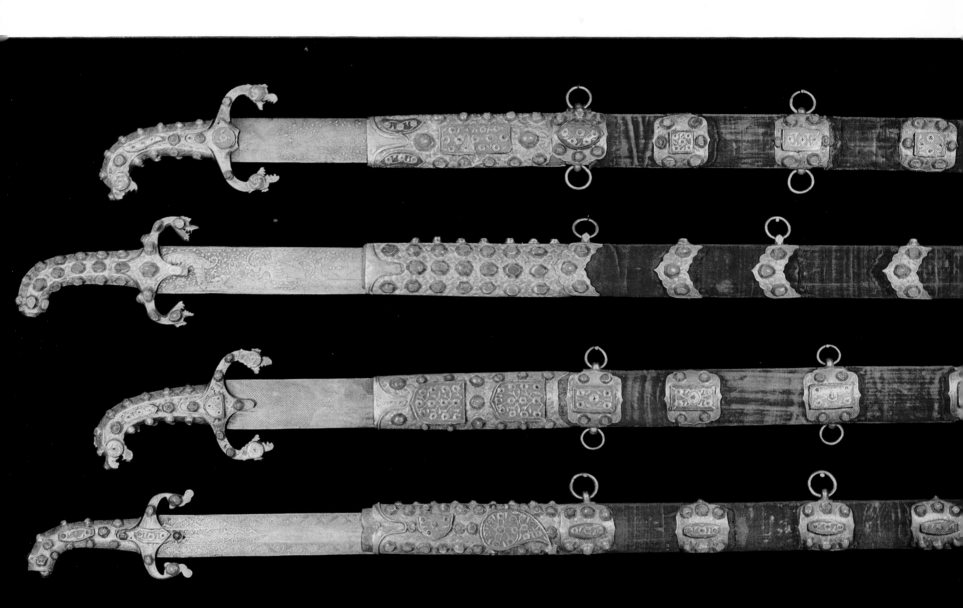

131. CEREMONIAL BROADSWORDS. 17TH CENTURY. ORIENT

132. THRONE OF TSAR
BORIS GODUNOV. LATE 16TH
CENTURY. IRAN

133. "DIAMOND" THRONE OF
TSAR ALEXEI MIKHAILOVICH.
1659. IRAN

134. "POKROVETS". 16TH CENTURY. DETAIL. IRAN

135. CAFTAN. LAST QUARTER 16TH CENTURY. IRAN ▶

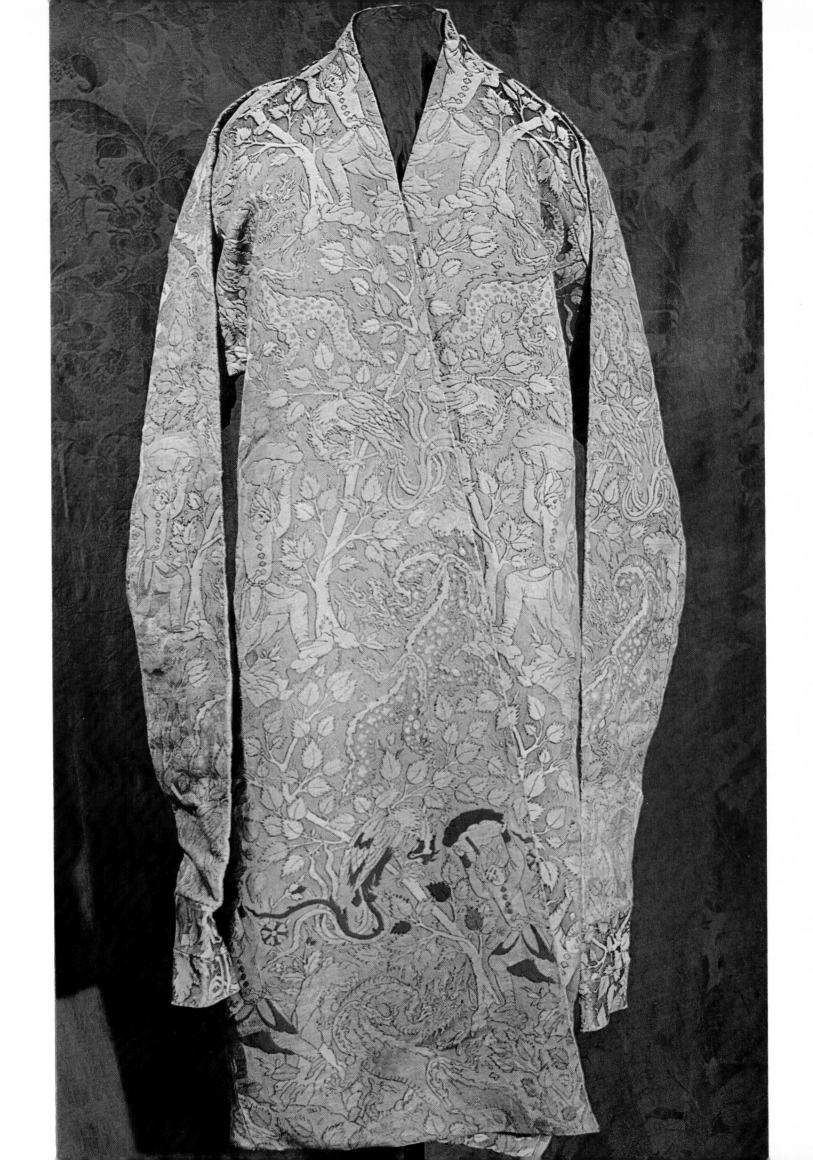

◄ 136. IRANIAN SADDLES AND HORSE-CLOTHES. 16TH—17TH CENTURY

137. SADDLE OF TSAR ALEXEI MIKHAILOVICH. SECOND HALF
17TH CENTURY. "CHALDAR". 17TH CENTURY. TURKEY

138. "SAADAK" OF TSAR ALEXEI MIKHAILOVICH. BOW CASE.
MID-17TH CENTURY. DETAIL. CONSTANTINOPLE. TURKEY ►

139. SAKKOS. 17TH CENTURY. TURKEY ►

WEST EUROPEAN ART
OF THE
15-19th
CENTURIES

THE COLLECTIONS of West-European applied art put the Moscow Armoury among the most important museums of the world. Their extent, the considerable period of time covered, wide range of the most important branches of artistic handicrafts, the clearly expressed national characteristics and the uniformly high standard of the items make the collection unique. The collection of arms and cold steel, accoutrements, textiles, tapestries, coaches, porcelain, glass, bone and silverware formed in different ways. The most important and interesting sections consist of items brought to Russia three or four hundred years ago as gifts of envoys.

Diplomatic etiquette which was established in its final form in Russia towards the end of the fifteenth and mid-sixteenth centuries and the ritual of presenting gifts occupied an important position. Gifts were treated as signs of respect for the state, greetings to the ruler, marks of attention from equals to equals, presents to ensure good will or good favour. They were carefully thought out and as a rule consisted of objects not merely of great intrinsic value, but of undoubted artistic import. Very often works were brought as gifts to Russia which were still novelties from the point of view of technical achievement or artistic taste in their own countries.

In the sixteenth-seventeenth centuries most European states presented silverware to the court of Ivan the Terrible or the first Romanovs. For sheer number of items, hardly any other European collection of such silverware can compare with the Armoury collection. This wealth of historical material, evidence of the many-sided diplomatic and trade relations between Russia and England, Holland, Denmark, Sweden, Germany, Austria and Poland, is the epitome of the major problems and stages of European diplomacy into whose orbit the Russian state was being drawn actively. At the same time it has undoubted educational and historic value. The collection of English silver is outstanding in importance. It is the biggest in the world but is remarkable not only for this fact. The highly individual features of every item are organically combined with the general national characteristics of the work of English silversmiths; furthermore, the artistic style of the time leaves its mark in each case. One examle is the silver gilt ewer (1594—1595), the work of John Morley of London. This collection relates roughly to the period from the mid-sixteenth to the mid-nineteenth centuries. The historical circumstances in which the collection was formed accounts for the unevenness of representation of various epochs and artistic trends. Most valuable from the historical and artistic point of view are the groups of silverware dating back to the 1580s and 1590s, the 1600s and 1604-1605 and the first half of the seventeenth century. They represent the Elizabethan silver and the early Baroque silver of the early Stuarts.

Mature English Baroque can be seen in the group of large gilded silver items dated 1663 and lavishly decorated with floral ornamentation. Eighteenth-nineteenth century silver is represented by a number of interesting individual items which illustrate Regency, and the English treatment of Rococo and Romanesque styles. Among the other national schools of silverware of continental Europe represented in the Armoury are the Dutch, German and French.

The collection of Dutch silver consists basically of gifts from envoys. It covers a well-defined period: the 1640s-1670s, a period that saw a great upsurge in Dutch art, big developments in painting, in a variety of *genres*, and the formation of various schools. It was a fruitful period for silverware which was caught up in the general renaissance.

There is a vast collection of German silver, consisting of a great number of items (over 1,000) the majority of which were gifts from envoys of various European countries. In the seventeenth century those states in which silversmithing was not so well developed would buy produce from famous German silversmiths to send to Russia as ambassadorial gifts. Denmark, Poland, Sweden and Austria usually acted in this way. But this was not the only manner in which German silver was amassed in the Moscow Treasury. The most important part of the present collection of silverware was bought by the Russian tsars. The biggest purchases were made by Tsar Mikhail Romanov at the Archangel International Fair in the 1620s. Another way in which silverware found its way to the Treasury was as presents from numerous citizens grateful for or seeking favours. The most popular and valuable gift of the seventeenth century and the one most assured of winning favour was a silver gilt cup, usually of German workmanship. The collection also includes silver handed over to the Armoury from other houses, such as that stored in the vaults of the Patriarch's Chambers.

As can be seen, the varied ways by which the collection of German silver came into existence are of historical interest, illuminating as they do many sides of the political, economic, cultural and dai y life of old Russia.

Silverware, being mainly items of daily use and at the same time works of art and objects of production, reflects the features, successes and changes and at times complex contradictions of the conditions which brought it into being. This makes German silver so interesting, and there is hardly any other collection of German silver that can supply such historic material. Practically all artistic centres of Germany are represented in the collection and by such high quality works of art and in such variety as enable one to get a comprehensive idea of the specific features of each artistic centre. A study of the collection shows the specialization in various kinds of silverware, the favourite decorative patterns and techniques, the development of forms and their changes, the evolution of styles from Gothic to Rococo, interrelations with other forms of art, and individual styles of master silversmiths.

If the collections of the Armoury were to be used to study changes in artistic trends in European applied art as a whole, then the collection of French silver would be most valuable in this respect, reflecting as it does various styles of the eighteenth-early nineteenth centuries. Items of the earlier period form a very small section of this collection. However, among them there is a real masterpiece of French silverware of the first half of the seventeenth century: a washing set comprising a ewer and basin. The eighteenth century, on the other hand, is represented by a large number of important works done by prominent Paris silversmiths.

It is interesting to know that the collection of silver reflects one of the features of the art of that period: the role played by outstanding painters, sculptors and architects in decorative art.

This phenomenon can be seen in other regions of applied art beside silverware, for example, in the important role of the painter François Boucher in decorating state coaches, such as the state coach of Catherine II.

The collection of West-European coaches is interesting because it illustrates the evolution of the technical side of coach building and decoration over a period of two centuries (sixteenth-eighteenth centuries). The coach builders of London, Paris, Vienna and Berlin are well represented. Coaches were often included among the gifts brought by foreign envoys to the court of Russian tsars. The oldest and most primitive of the coaches in the collection is the sixteenth-early seventeenth century English coach. A more advanced vehicle is the early seventeenth century coach of Polish make. The eighteenth century is indeed well represented in the collection.

Among other West-European art collections of the Armoury on a world level, those of textiles and field armour are worthy of attention.

The armour made by West-European masters goes back to the fifteenth-seventeenth centuries. The majority of the armour exhibited in the Museum was made for tournaments, and was rather for decorative than for military purpose.

Of the hand-woven textiles produced in Europe during the fourteenth-eighteenth centuries the place of honour goes to the collection of Italian velvets, the biggest in the world. The textile is basically of fine silk, usually red, green or yellow, with a thread of spun gold used in the weft, which gave the cloth a luxurious look. The best velvets were made in Venice. In the seventeenth century they were very heavy and close-woven. Five metres of such fabric, enough for one set of raiments, weigh about sixteen kilograms. The 1654 sakkos of Patriarch Nicon was made of specially splendid double uncut velvet. In addition, it was oversewn with pearls, precious stones and gold pieces, and weighed almost twenty-four kilograms.

This rich cloth first appeared at the Moscow court in the middle of the seventeenth century and made a deep impression. Velvet was imitated in embroidery and influenced the traditional Russian range of patterns.

When European dress became fashionable in Russia at the beginning of the eighteenth century French textiles, especially silks and brocades woven in Lyons, found their way into Russia. They are well represented. Rare samples of Spanish brocades are a particularly interesting part of the collection.

West-European armour is represented by a group of field armour and tournament accoutrements, helmets, and arms worn on special occasions in the fifteenth-eighteenth centuries. Brought to Russia as rarities of no practical application, these items were usually intended for and specially ordered as presents to Russian tsars and nobility. An interesting example of this kind of armour is the helmet made by the famous master Lucio Piccinino of Milan, which bears the Moscow coat of arms.

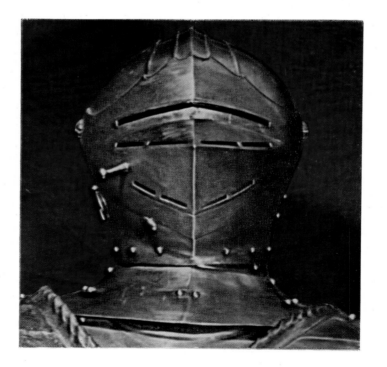

140. TOURNAMENT ARMOUR . 15TH CENTURY. HELMET. GERMANY
141. TOURNAMENT ARMOUR. 15TH CENTURY. GERMANY ▶

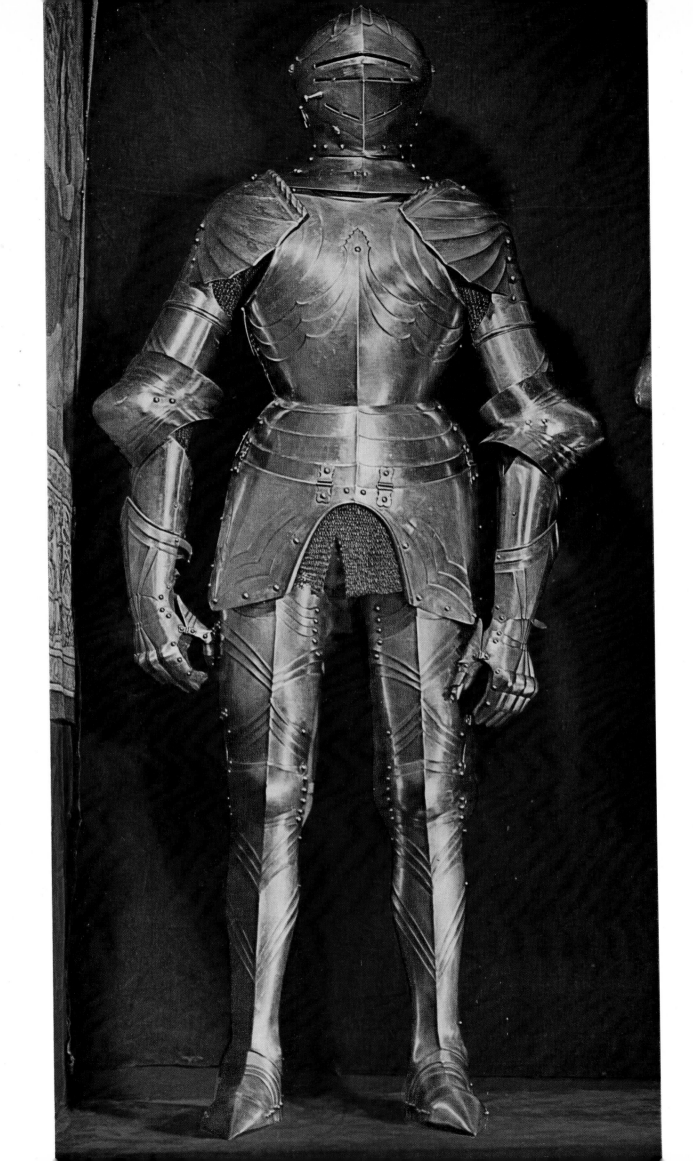

142. CHALICE. LATE 15TH CENTURY. GERMANY   143. "DÜRER" TYPE GOBLET. LATE 15TH—EARLY 16TH CENTURY. NUREMBERG. GERMANY

144. BASIN. MADE BY TOBIAS KRAMER (ACTIVE 1615-34). AUGSBURG, GERMANY

145. INTERIOR OF COACH HALL
146. WEST-EUROPEAN SADDLES AND HORSE-CLOTHES. 16TH—17TH CENTURY ▶

147, 148. HELMET. MADE BY LUCIO PICCININO (ACTIVE 1550—1600). MILAN, ITALY

151. COACH OF PATRIARCH FILARET. EARLY 17TH CENTURY. POLAND

151. COACH OF PATRIARCH FILARET. EARLY 17TH CENTURY. POLAND

152. "KOLYMAGA" OF TSAR BORIS GODUNOV. LATE 16TH—EARLY 17TH CENTURY

153. EWER FOR HAND-WASHING ("VORONOK"). MADE BY JOHN MORLEY (?). 1594-5. LONDON, ENGLAND

154. BASIN. LATE 16TH CENTURY. LONDON, ENGLAND

155. SAKKOS OF PATRIARCH PARTHENIUS OF CONSTANTINOPLE. 1643. SPAIN ▶

156. EWER FOR HAND-WASHING. MADE BY CRAFTSMAN WITH MONOGRAM R. C. PARIS, FRANCE
157. EWER. MADE BY JEAN ODIOT. 1809-19. PARIS, FRANCE

158. SURPLICE. LATE 17TH—EARLY 18TH CENTURY. FRAGMENT. FRANCE

159. BASIN. MADE BY CRAFTSMAN WITH HALL-MARK "STALKING LION". 1625 or 1649. PARIS. FRANCE

160, 161, 162, 163. CEREMONIAL CAFTANS AND CAMISOLES OF EMPEROR PETER II. FIRST HALF 18TH CENTURY. FRANCE

◄ 164. COACH OF EMPRESS ELIZAVETA PETROVNA. MADE BY BOURNIHALL. MINIATURES BY F. BOUCHER. MID-18TH CENTURY. FRANCE

165. DECORATIVE DISH. MADE BY CRAFTSMAN WITH MONOGRAM N. T. c. 1665. AMSTERDAM, HOLLAND

RUSSIAN ART
OF THE
18-19 th
CENTURIES

T THE CLOSE of the seventeenth and the beginning of the eighteenth century Russian culture was undergoing a change of enormous historical importance: the period of medieval art was coming to an end and a new, secular art, basically realistic, was being born.

A fundamental rearrangement of the state apparatus enabled Peter the Great to create an entirely new type of Russian state and turn Moscow Rus into a Russian Empire. In the eighteenth century Russia was transformed into a mighty state which held one of the first places among the advanced powers in the Europe of that time. The growth of productive forces, the development of industry and expansion of trade relations led to a new upsurge of science and culture in the country. The eighteenth century was marked by new successes in art made possible by the artistic achievements of previous centuries. Russian art, developing as it did in the main stream of the art of West-European countries, nevertheless preserved its national character. St Petersburg became the centre of the economic, political and cultural life of the country.

The activities of the art workshops at the Moscow Kremlin proved to be quite contrary to the new state policy. They were producing objects which, in the main, had no direct practical application. Peter the Great put an end to all this. The woodcarvers of the Armoury were sent to Voronezh and Archangel in 1696-9 where they were expected to decorate the ships built there. In 1711 all the best master craftsmen of the Moscow Kremlin workshops were sent to St Petersburg to work at the newly founded Armoury there, which manufactured arms and "all kinds of fitters' and turners' lathes", since because of the outbreak of the Northern War the Armoury was concentrating mostly on supplying the Russian army with all kinds of fire arms and cold steel. The work of serving the court and its needs was considered of secondary importance. The decrees of Peter the Great placing restrictions on use of gold and silver by individuals led to a general reduction in the production of jewellery and similar objects.

In 1722 guilds of gold and silversmiths were formed. Moscow had occupied a leading position in the production of silverware to start with, but little by little St Petersburg replaced Moscow in quality of silverware, too, because the best craftsmen were to be found in St Petersburg from the middle of the eighteenth century. Up to the 1740s Russian silver, both in design and in decoration, was still closely akin to that of the seventeenth century. But from the middle of the eighteenth century both the shape of the objects and their ornamentation changed decisively. Entirely new designs appeared.

During the eighteenth century, depending on which style was fashionable at a particular time, the following techniques came to the fore in turn: casting and incising, chasing and niello, filigree and enamel. The painted enamel which replaced various enamel techniques of the seventeenth century was particularly highly developed. It was wide-spread in the eighteenth and nineteenth centuries, only its colour range changing with time. At that time craftsmen hardly ever covered the whole object with enamel. More often than not only small areas were picked out in enamel as part of the decoration. The surface of the areas covered with enamel ground was worked over with enamel paints diluted with turpentine and applied with soft brushes. The next step was firing. This process was repeated several times, depending on the complexity of the colour range used. Comparatively simple in technique and at the same time allowing for great decorative freedom, painted enamel found wide usage in decorations of various religious and secular objects: caskets, snuff-boxes, watches, covers for the gospels, chalices and the like.

The colours in these painted enamels were usually those of precious stones. The bright colours used on the Rococo objects were echoed by bright green emeralds, cornflower blue sapphires and rich red rubies. The objects done in Russian classical style and painted with *grisaille* enamel were usually decorated with pale mauve amethysts and azure blue aquamarines. The most valuable objects of that period, those of the greatest artistic interest, were often covered completely with diamonds. In the 1720s the mineral riches of the Urals were intensively worked. The best kinds of amethysts, sapphires, topazes, alexandrites, aquamarines, avanturines, and other precious and semi-precious stones were obtained there.

Enamel and precious stones were used most often to embellish the pectoral insignia of the high priests: the panagias, and also snuff-boxes, which had become very popular among the Russian feudal nobility of the time in connection with the unrestricted sale of tobacco and the consequent fashion of snuff-taking.

The eighteenth-nineteenth century panagias are extremely varied in shape and style of decoration. Some were in the form of a cross, emanating radiance, others were oval or rhomboid in form, yet others were made in the form of rosettes or rich garlands surrounding enamelled medallions. The richest and most beautiful were the panagias presented by the Royal Family, the reverse of which often bore miniatures of Russian Empresses.

The development of enamelled miniatures was closely connected with the development of Russian easel painting. One of the founders of the Russian school of portrait painting, L. Antropov, for example, was at the same time an enamel miniaturist.

In decorating snuff-boxes the craftsmen's fancy was given free reign. Round or oval, oblong or octagonal in shape, deep or shallow, executed in gold or silver, ivory and tortoise shell, porcelain or semi-precious stones, they were often in amazingly fine artistic taste and clearly done with supreme professional skill. The snuff boxes, which were used as royal gifts or awards, were made with special attention to detail and richness of ornament. Like the panagias which were used for royal gifts, they usually bore miniatures of royalty or their monograms worked in diamonds.

Among the eighteenth century jewellers I. Posier and G. Ador were the best known, their fame having spread to other countries too.

The changes which took place in the domestic life of Russian feudal nobility following the reforms of Peter the Great led to old traditional costumes being replaced by clothes made in West-European fashion. Women started wearing low-cut gowns with long trains. Men—short, knee-length breeches, waistcoats, and close-fitting, knee-length coats with flaring skirts. One of the earliest examples of European type clothes are the coronation robe of Catherine I and the coats of Peter II, whose entire wardrobe is preserved in the Armoury. The robe of Catherine I is made of vermilion silk with splendid silver embroidery.

By the middle of the eighteenth century hoop skirts became fashionable. The wedding dress of Catherine II is a typical example of this style. It was made of silver cloth richly embroidered in silver thread.

The late eighteenth-early nineteenth century saw another change in the fashion for high society: under the influence of the ideas of the French bourgeois revolution and the newly acquired love for Greek antiquity, dresses made of bright textiles such as brocade and silk with hoops and lace flounces and gold and silver embroidery were replaced by tunic-like dresses made of light transparent materials mainly white in colour.

With the considerable diminution of the pearl trade and the introduction of West-European dress, the use of pearls declined sharply in the eighteenth century. Pearls continued to be used only in objects for secular purposes.

As a consequence pearl embroidery suffered and deteriorated to a standard below that of the sixteenth-seventeenth centuries though there are some examples, remarkable for their time, of great artistic taste. For example, the Armoury has a whole set comprising the gift made in 1770 to the Trinity-Sergius Lavra by Catherine II. However, the pearls for this gift were taken from the gowns and icon clothes of the sixteenth-seventeenth centuries, many of which were gifts from Ivan the Terrible, Boris Godunov and other historical personalities.

The patterns of pearl embroidery in the eighteenth century usually repeated the patterns of the then fashionable textiles, and also the ornaments of gold and silverware. Expecially popular were designs of clusters of grapes and roses. Pearl embroidery included crown and monogram patterns which acquired independent artistic importance. These were all signs of the strong influence of secular on ecclesiastical art.

One of the rooms of the State Armoury displays valuable wall hangings made by the tapestry workshop in St Petersburg (tapestries were made in St Petersburg between 1717 and 1859). The most beautiful of them were woven in the second half of the eighteenth century when the workshop employed Russian weavers in the main.

Russian eighteenth-nineteenth century applied and decorative art, despite the fact that it developed in forms identical to the European styles of the time, differed considerably from them in the bright and cheerful colour range of the objects, its more full-blooded and realistic images and their generally cheerful tone. Throughout one feels constant profound ties with Russian folk art. Created by master craftsmen from among the people, who rejected both the dry mannerisms and the over-indulgence in stylization characteristic of West-European art, Russian decorative and applied art of the eighteenth century fully preserved its national features.

166. ARRAS. 1735. FRAGMENT
167. ARRAS. 1735 ▶

170. SNUFF-BOX. 1780. MADE BY G. ADOR. MINIATURE MADE BY C. GEYER

171. SNUFF-BOX. 1764. MADE BY G. ADOR

172. PANAGIA. 1767

173. PHELONION. 1770. EMBROIDERED BY D. LIKHNOVSKAYA ▶

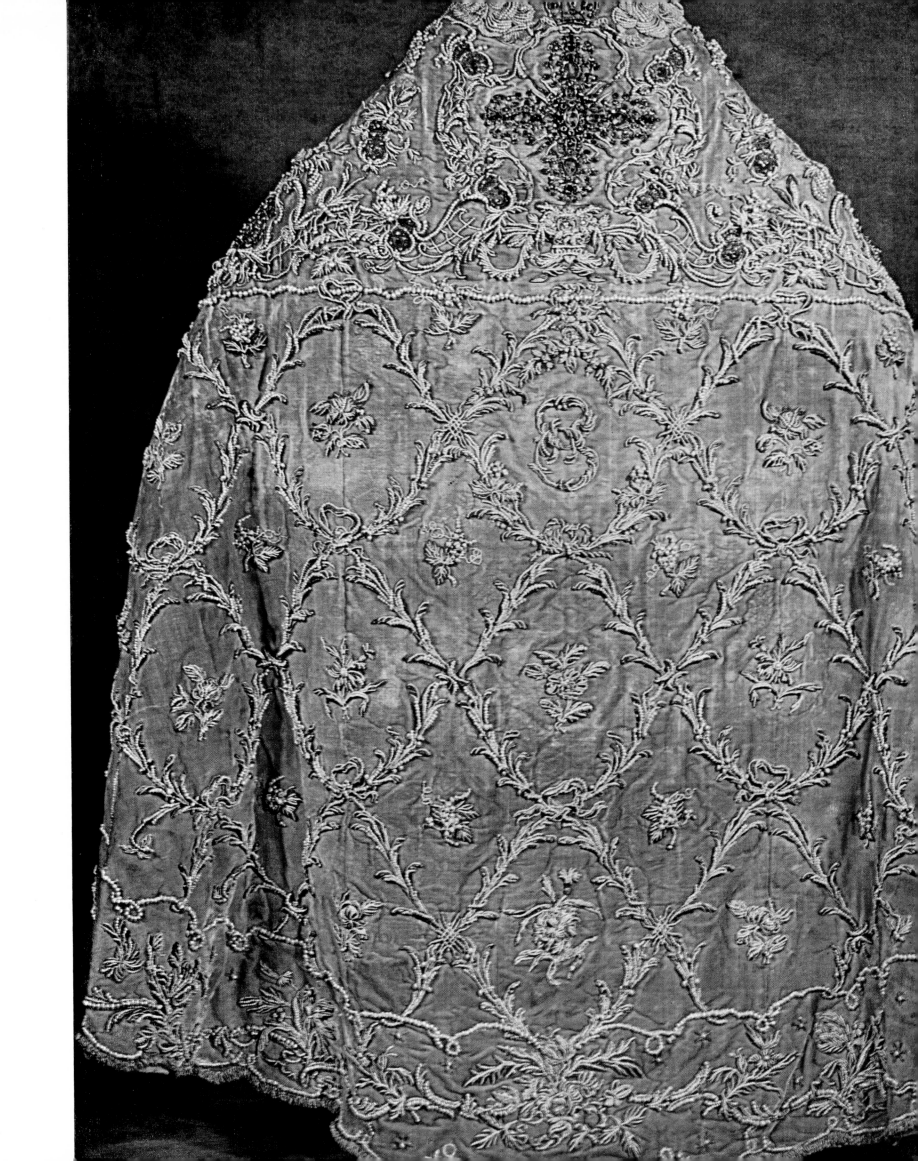

◄ 174. CORONATION ROBES. 19TH CENTURY
175. INTERIOR OF COACH HALL

C O M M E N T A R Y

RUSSIAN ART OF 12TH-15TH CENTURIES

1,2. HELMET OF PRINCE YAROSLAV VSEVOLODOVICH OF PERESLAVL-ZALESSKY. LATE 12TH-EARLY 13TH CENTURY. VLADIMIR-SUZDAL RUS

Iron, silver. Chasing, forging
Height 21 cm; diameter 18 cm
Came from A. I. Olenin (1763-1843), the President of the Academy of Fine Arts, in 1843
Discovered in 1808 by peasants at a bank of the Koloksha River near Yuriev-Polsky, Vladimir Region

The helmet was discovered at the place of the Lipetsk battle (1216) waged between the sons of Vsevolod the Great Nest (1177-1212), the prince of Vladimir. Constantine and George (Yuri) struggled for the throne of the Grand Princes of Vladimir. Prince George was supported by his brother Yaroslav (1191-1246) The victory was won by Constantine, while George and Yaroslav took to flight from the battlefield, leaving their weapons It is possible, though, that the helmet, made for the teenager, was too small for the Prince Yaroslav who came now to man's estate, and was hidden in a secret place before the beginning of the battle The helmet was to be discovered only six hundred years later.

The helmet is hammered from a single sheet of iron. Its surface is polished and ornamented with plates of *repoussé* silver. The front of the helmet is decorated with a plaque with the Archangel Michael The plaque is bordered with an inscription in niello: "The great Archistrategus Michael, help Feodor, your servant" Yaroslav Vsevolodovich was baptized Feodor, so Russian Princes usually had several names. The lower part of the helmet's crown and the nose-guard are pierced with holes for fixing a special necklace made of iron rings. Some historians date the helmet to earlier times and connect it with the name of Mstislav Yurievich, Prince of Novgorod (1154-7), the younger son of Yuri Dolgoruky, who was also baptized Feodor. However, some facts prove that Mstislav Yurievich couldn't have been the possessor of the helmet.

3. "BARMY" OF GRAND PRINCES. 12TH-13TH CENTURY. KIEVAN RUS

Gold, gems, pearls. Cloisonné enamel, filigree, granulation
Diameter of medallions 74-80 cm; length of bead 4 cm
Originated from the "Staro-Ryazan Treasure". Discovered in 1822 in the place where Staraya Ryazan was

The "barmy" is a kind of a necklace made of pendant medallions linked in a string by open-worked beads. "Barmy", the sign of power of the Grand Princes, at that age belonged to the family of the Grand Princes and were worn over their ceremonial luxurious robes, embroidered with gold, pearls and silks. The obverse of the round gold medallions is covered with a thick layer of manytiered light filigree, making a beautiful design of thin stylized branches and flowers, twisted into small spiral curves. The design is sprinkled with the finest drops of granulation to make it more beautiful. The three central medallions have the images of the Virgin, SS Irene and Barbara in *cloisonné* enamel. They are bordered with vertical Russian inscriptions.

The medallions are inset with blue and green sapphires and light-red garnets, with pearls encircled them. The reverse side of the medallions is plain. To produce such a work of art was a dificult and complicated process

4. SMALL ICON "ST DEMETRIUS OF THESSALONICA". 13TH-14TH CENTURY

Gilded silver, stone. Casting, chasing, carving
Heigth (with top) 9.3 cm; width of base 9.6 cm
Came from the Annunciation Cathedral in the Moscow Kremlin in 1931

The cast image of St Demetrius of Thessalonica is laid on a pectoral icon in gilded silver setting
In the 13th-14th century, among the saint warriors and heroes of spiritual poems and folk legends, SS George and Demetrius were usually found on such icons, because of their popularity during the period of the Tartar-Mongolian yoke, the hardest for the Russian people.

Unlike the usual canonical image, St Demetrius holds not a spear but a banner
The setting is ornamented with carved images of saints and inscriptions. The reverse is plain.

5,6,7. TRIPTYCH. MADE BY LUCIAN. 1412. VLADIMIR-SUZDAL RUS

Gilded silver, pearls. Niello, chasing, carving
Height with top 10.1 cm; with open folds 13.5 cm; width of base with closed folds 7.1 cm
Came from the Annunciation Cathedral in the Moscow Kremlin
To all probability it belonged to Prince of Suzdal-Nizhni Novgorod. When these lands had been joined to the Principality of Moscow in the early 15th century, their wealth has got into the Treasury of the Grand Princes of Moscow

In the central part of the open triptych is the *repoussé* image of the Saviour Enthroned in the deepened icon-case. Christ has gilded hair, beard and himation, as on the early Russian icons. The surface between the arch and the icon-case, as well as the edges of the central portion of the triptych, have a frame of open-work cut branches of the Tree of Life, the favourite theme of early Slavonic art. On the left fold, above, is the image of the Archangel Michael, below are the Virgin and St John the Forerunner; on the right fold, above, is the Crucifixion, below are the Holy Women. Though the triptych is small, the slightest details may be distinguished, as the keys in St Peter's hands, vessels kept by the Holy Women, ornamentation and folds of clothes, etc. The artist expresses individuality in every person with exceptional mastership.

The obverse of the central portion pictures in roundels St Nicholas, St Demetrius of Thessalonica, Elijah the Prophet, Cosmus the Healer, and an Angel This meant to show that St Demetrius was the inspirer of warriors, St Cosmus the doctor. Princes took this icon when going to war, to be safe from illnesses and disasters.

The top of the triptych is decorated with symbols of Life and Death as two counterveiling faces, and with the carved inscription:
"Death—Life". Life wins a victory over death, is the idea of the triptych. The *repoussé* inscription at the butt end of the folds tells that the triptych was made in 1412 by the craftsman Lucian.

8. HELMET WITH IRON-CLAD NECKLACE. 14TH CENTURY. MADE BY MOSCOW CRAFTSMEN

Hammered iron
Height with spire 45 cm; diameter 23 cm; weight with necklace 12.0 kg
From the basic collection. Indexed in 1685

The helmet is hammered from a single sheet of iron. Its surface has straight flutes, the top is pointed to a long spire where a red flag ("yalovets") was usually fixed.

The wide plane brim of the helmet has holes for fixing an iron-clad necklace defending from arrows and sabre blows. The face was covered with an iron netting, used by warriors to observe the enemy from behind the castellated walls in the 12th-14th century.

9,10,11. BOAR-SPEAR OF TVER PRINCE BORIS ALEXANDROVICH. 15TH CENTURY

Damask steel silver Forging, polishing, carving
Length 46 cm; diameter of tube 4.6 cm
From the basic collection. Indexed in 1685
The boar-spear is indexed in the most ancient inventory of the Tsar Treasury. Probably it was a property of Ivan III Vassilievich (1440-1505), the Grand Prince of Moscow, after his marriage with Maria, daughter of Boris Alexandrovich, the independent Prince of Tver

The edges of the tube are ornamented with the following inscription: "The boar-spear of the Grand Prince Boris Alexandrovich", who ruled in Tver during 1425-61.
The boar-spear is forged from excellent Damask steel; its short tetrahedral hook ends in an octahedral tube with engraved silver plates. The tube used to be hafted on a long oak shaft. The carved octahedral tube respresents eight hunting scenes. Every scene takes up two facets of the tube.

12. MOUNTING OF ICON "THE VIRGIN OF VLADIMIR". 13TH CENTURY. DETAIL. VLADIMIR-SUZDAL RUS

Gold. "Basma", chasing
Size of mounting: height 1.05 cm; width 70 cm
Came from the Patriarch Vestry in 1920

The icon "The Virgin of Vladimir" (State Tretyakov Gallery), made in Byzantium in the early 12th century, was brought from Constantinople to Moscow in 1136. Since 1480 it was kept in the Dormition Cathedral in the Moscow Kremlin. The icon was much revered in Russia and, according to the customs, was bordered with a luxurious mounting. Several precious mountings were made for this icon, three of them are kept in the Armoury. The present mounting is the earliest. It is made of golden plaques with the "basma" braided ornament, typical for early Russian art of the period. The upper part is embossed in rather high relief with the Deesis Range. Figures of Christ, St John the Forerunner and the Archangel Gabriel are magnificent and imposing. The images are treated in pure Russian style, even an inscription in *repoussé* above St John's head is written in Russian characters: "Иванъ" ("Ivan"). The simple way and noble calm of every figure and the whole composition resemble the outlines of the white-stone cathedrals of Vladimir-Suzdal Rus.

13. CHALICE OF PRINCE YURI DOLGORUKY. MID-12TH CENTURY. VLADIMIR-SUZDAL RUS

Silver, partly gilded. Chasing, carving
Height 26 cm; diameter of bowl 19.5 cm
Came from the Transfiguration Cathedral in Pereslavl-Zalessky in 1931. Contribution of Prince Yuri Dolgoruky (c. 1090-1157), founder of Moscow, into the Transfiguration Cathedral built in 1152

This silver chalice (a cup for wine of the Holy Communion) is a unique precious relic of applied art of the 12th century Vladimir-Suzdal Rus. The chalice is simple, strict and, at the same time, fine and noble. Not great in size, the specimen produces the impression of a magnificent vessel. Its plain, semi-spherical wide cup is ornamented with carved figures of the Deesis Range, and among them there is St George as a curly youth, in the clothes of a partician. The image of St George who was the personal patron of the Prince Yuri Dolgoruky, allows to date the chalice from the mid-12th century. The liturgical inscription carved on the edges of the bowl ("Drink ye all of it for this is my blood") is made very clear and fine. The style of the inscription comports with the images of the saints on the chalice, as well as with the other relics of the period. The broad, heavy *repoussé* stand is worked in spoon-shaped depressions, with ribbed acanthus leaves between. The leaves on the lower, wide part are worked in *repoussé*, at the, upper, narrower one they are carved.

14,15. GREAT ZION. 1486. WORKSHOPS OF THE MOSCOW KREMLIN

Silver. Niello, chasing, carving
Height 94 cm
Came from the Patriarch Vestry in 1920
Made by Moscow silversmiths in 1846 to order of the Great Prince of Moscow Ivan III Vassilievich (1462-1505). Intended for the church ceremonies in the Dormition Cathedral in the Moscow Kremlin

The Great Zion is a large decorative shrine in the shape of a cathedral, with a floor adorned with ogee arches, with a cut drum, an onion-like dome crowned with a cross and decorated with birds, fishes, human faces and heads of animals. The lower part of the shrine has the shape of a rotund with round nielloed columns; in the arches, between them, there are the twelve apostles, embossed in high relief.
Some details were made not at the same time, so the work is of different styles. Probably, the shrine was made up of silver tabernacles of the 12th century (from the cathedrals of Vladimir). It is known that in 1846 Moscow craftsmen made the floor, the dome, the background behind the Apostles anew, as well as the carved ornamentations and inscriptions, nimbi of the saints, and columns and arches; all this was adorned with niello. The solid, big-headed and short-legged figures of the apostles are, probably, of Western work and differ in proportions and expression from the vivid figures of the four prophets.

16,17. ICON "THE VIRGIN ELEUSA" IN MOUNTING. 14TH CENTURY MOUNTING. 12TH-13TH CENTURY ORPHREYS IN CLOISONNÉ ENAMEL

Tempera on lime board. Silver, gold, gems, pearls. Cloisonné enamel, chasing, filigre
Height 41.6 cm; width 32.7 cm
Came from the Cathedral of the Archangel Michael in the Moscow Kremlin in 1919

The mounting of the icon is of a rare and precious type of relics in Russian applied art of the 12th-14th century. The *repoussé* mounting and its several ornamentations are made in the early Russian traditions. The solid vegetation ornamentation embossed in high relief forms double heart-shaped control stamps in the lower and upper parts of the mounting. In the centre of every control stamp is a big trefoliate flower made in the style of "krin" (from the Greek "krinon", "lily") which was very popular in Russian ornamentations of the 14th century and later (in the 16th-17th century). The *repoussé* orphreys of the 12th-13th century made in *cloisonné* enamel are bordered with the *repoussé* dots, stamped at the verso.
The 13th century icon-painting was partly restored and even repainted during the 19th century

18. CENSER OF PRINCE YURI VASSILIEVICH. 1469

Gilded silver. Chasing, carving, forging
Height 28 cm; diameter of bowl 12.3 cm
Acquired from the Commission of the Church Property Reception of the Museum Department of the People Educational Commissariat in 1920
The censer was contributed by the Prince Yuri Vassilievich, son of the Grand Prince of Moscow Vassili II the Blind (1425-62), into the Nikolo-Peshnoshsky Monastery (near Dmitrov) in 1469

The lower plain semi-spherical bowl with its rich soft gilding distinguishes for its peculiar gentle shimmering (because of long and scrupulous metal forging) which imparts so much charm to early Russian utensils. At the upper edge of the bowl is engraved an inscription referring to the contribution of the censer. At the early 17th century the censer was probably reworked, and only the lower plain bowl and the dome of the drum date from 1469. The upper part of the censer reproduces the ribbed hip floor with two sloping surfaces of an early Russian cathedral of rare beauty and originality. In its lower part on cut facets are soldered small icon-cases with cast figures of the Deesis Range, two in each icon-case. The hip-roof could be dated from the first quarter of the 16th century

19. PANAGIA. 15TH CENTURY. MADE IN WORKSHOPS OF THE MOSCOW KREMLIN

Gilded silver. Chasing, niello, enamel, carving, casting
Diameter 14.5 cm
Acquired in 1923. Formerly in the Kirillo-Belozersky Monastery where it was probably granted by someone of Grand Princes of Moscow or by Metropolitan of Moscow

The panagia is a pectoral plate intended for the high priesthood. The Greek word "pan-agia" means "all-sacred". Panagias were used for different occasions. The present panagia was called "the travelling" ("putnaya"). Starting on a journey, the priests usually took such panagias along with the so-called "the Virgin bread" ("Bogorodichny"). The panagia is made of two round shell-like folds on a hinge. The obverse of the upper fold is adorned with "The Ascension", consisted of the eight separately casted figures on the nielloed background. This ecclesiastical theme is often seen on similar panagias at the late 14th-early 15th century. The inner sides of the folds were usually ornamented with the carved image of the Virgin Blacherniotissa or with "The Trinity".

20. CHALICE OF ARCHBISHOP MOSES OF NOVGOROD 1329. NOVGOROD

Jasper, gilded silver, gems. Chasing, carving, filigree
Came from the Annunciation Cathedral in the Moscow Kremlin in 1922

The plain and expressive form of the chalice, the fine combination of gilded filigree mounting, ornamented with semi-precious stones and fretwork, with the deep-red jasper of the bowl allows to qualify the chalice as an excellent masterpiece of church utensils made by the best jewellers of early Russia. The plain wide edge of the bowl is ornamented with an engraved liturgical inscription, traditional for chalices: "Drink ye all of it"... The characters belong to the earliest type of the Slavonic handwriting, and amid the inscription are the six carved medallions with half-figures of the Deesis Range. Diverging from the usual rules of disposing saints in the Deesis, St Moses is the sixth, for he was the personal patron of the chalice customer. Unlike the Archangels, the St Moses's bust is engirdled with a magnificent carved frame. Below the chalice's edges an inscription tells that this vessel was made to order of the Archbishop Moses in 1329

21.22. GOSPELS OF METROPOLITAN SIMON OF MOSCOW. COVER. 1499.
MADE IN WORKSHOPS OF THE MOSCOW KREMLIN

Gilded silver. Enamel, filigree, niello, chasing, casting, carving
Height 32 cm; width 22 cm
Came from the Patriarch Vestry in 1920
Formerly in the Dormition Cathedral in the Moscow Kremlin; contributed by
the Metropolitan Simon of Moscow and All Russia in 1499

The central portion of the cover in the shape of a small keel-like arch on
pillars is covered with emerald-green enamel that forms the background
for "The Crucifixion with Interceding Saints". The Evangelists are disposed in the keel-shaped cast icon-cases. The central narrow long plaques
at the top and bottom of the cover are adorned with a carved inscription
in the Slavonic decorative writing referring to the producing of the Gospels under the Grand Prince Ivan III (1462-1505).
The cover of the Gospels is the best specimen of the filigree mastership in
early Russia, at the end of the 15th century. The obverse is covered with
rich lace of filigree ornament, exceedingly fine and light. The general
pattern is made of plain wire flattened out, while the small tendrils,
curves and loops are made of the finest twisted wire.
The manuscript of the Gospels written on paper is decorated with beautiful
colour illuminations and initials.

23,24,25. SAKKOS OF METROPOLITAN ALEXIUS OF MOSCOW. 1364

Ornamentation in pearls of Russian work
Damask, wire-drawn gold and silver, pearls. Cloisonné enamel, gilding, niello, carving
Length 122 cm; width (with sleeves) 132 cm. Cuffs: height 17 cm; length 91 cm
Came from the Chudov Monastery

The yoke, short sleeves and hem of the sakkos are decorated with silver
gilt plates and Russian river pearls. The twisted pearl stalk embroidered on
the yoke is typical for Byzantine art, and Russian craftsmen used it in various patterns of embroideries and ornamentation of gold- and silverware,
till the early 18th century. Large crosses and angels are embroidered on the
blue Damask field of the sakkos; they make the "crescent" pattern similar
to the patterns on Byzantine tissues. The silver gilt orphreys of the 12th-
13th century, ornamented with Russian *cloisonné* enamel, are of great value; they are applied to the sleeves and the hem, as well as between the
crosses.
The sakkos (long tunic with short sleeves and round collar) is a vestment of
high priesthood.

26. STOLE OF METROPOLITAN ALEXIUS OF MOSCOW. SECOND HALF 14TH
CENTURY. DETAIL

Ornamentation in pearls of Russian work
Satin, gilded silver, pearls. Cloisonné enamel, niello, gilding
Length 105.0 cm; width 30.0 cm
Came from the Chudov Monastery

This stole is a rare masterpiece of Russian ornamentation in pearls. The
large round orphreys of the 12th-13th century are the central point of the
composition. They are decorated with the busts of saints in *cloisonné*
enamel. The orphreys interchange alternately with pearl rosettes. The sys-
tematical arrangement of pattern is stressed by small plain plates in the
shape of leaves flanking the orphreys. They seem to emerge from the narrow
ornamental bands on the edges of the stole and make the composition
very expressive and shapely.

27,28. ARMLETS OF METROPOLITAN ALEXIUS OF MOSCOW. ORPHREYS
1354-78

Ornamentation in pearls of Russian work
Satin, gilded silver, pearls. Cloisonné enamel, gilding
Orphreys: height 5 cm; length 5 cm
Came from the Chudov Monastery

The silver gilded orphreys are the most remarkable in the embroidering
of the sleeves. One orphrey is ornamented with a plant-geometrical pattern
in *cloisonné* enamel; the other is adorned with the Tree of Life with flanking birds
These designs, so popular in early Russian art, in particular the Tree of
Life, may be found in embroidery, lace, wood carving and stone engraving.
Every orphrey, encircled by pearls of middle size and a thick gilded
twisted thread ("truntsal"), is confined into a diamond-shaped frame
made of small orphreys in *cloisonné* enamel, also bordered with pearls.

29. "MOROZOV" GOSPELS. COVER. FIRST THIRD 15TH CENTURY. MADE
IN WORKSHOPS OF MOSCOW KREMLIN

Gold, gems, pearls. Filigree, chasing
Height 39 cm; width 30 cm
Came from the Patriarch Vestry of Moscow in 1920
Text and miniatures made by order of the Metropolitan Photius of Moscow for the
Dormition Cathedral in the Moscow Kremlin

This Gospels book, named the "Morozov" Gospels, was supposed to be a
contribution of the Boyard B.I. Morozov (1590-1661) in the Dormition
Cathedral in the Moscow Kremlin, yet it was made in the first third of the
15th century to order of the Moscow Metropolitan Photius. The Gospels were
only restored to order of B.I. Morozov in the 1660s, though they were always called the "Morozov" Gospels.
The Gospels have reached our days almost intact and is considered as one
of the rarest precious works of early Russian art. The rich cover and the
beautiful manuscript of the Gospels were made almost simultaneously.
The cover of the Gospels is the unique gold cover of the first half of the 15th
century. It is patterned with rich filigree ornament soldered on convex
plaques. Between the filigree ornamentation there are uncut gems in casts
and the *repoussé* images of the Apostles, angels, cherubim and "Fathers of
the Church". In the centre of the cover is the traditional composition
"The Descent into Hell", with symbols of the Evangelists in the corners.

30. "MOROZOV" GOSPELS. FRONTISPIECE OF GOSPEL OF ST JOHN. FIRST
THIRD 15TH CENTURY. ANDREI RUBLEV SCHOOL

Tempera on parchment
Size of leaf: height 35.5 cm; width 29 cm
Size of illumination: height 12.8 cm; width 19 cm

The text of the Gospels is written on 365 leaves of parchment, in large liturgical characters, in two columns.
Its ornamentation is typical to the 15th century: seven illuminations,
eight miniatures with the Evangelists and their symbols, and a great
quantity of initials in the shape of intangled serpents, winged fantastical
dragons, birds and various other animals.
The manuscript, as well as the decorations, are no doubt the works of great
artists. The exclusive finesse, the delicate shades of colour, light drawings
and the calm seen on every leaf render the composition complete and finish-
ed. The ornament of the illumination is made in the so-called "neo-Byzantine" style, well-known after the Greek manuscripts of the 10th century
and these of Russia of the 11th-12th century: the symmetrical roundels
with plant ornament on a golden field. At the late 14th century this
style was brought to many parts of Russia.
The illumination of the "Morozov" Gospels is rectangular, with flowers
(on one side) and two birds before a bowl (above), which is the diversion
from the "neo-Byzantine" style. The manuscript is written in the scrupulous
solemn writing; the characters are in a fine-hand. Every leaf of the Gospels
seems to be a complete work of art.

31,32. "MOROZOV" GOSPELS. MINIATURES. FIRST THIRD 15TH CENTURY
ANDREI RUBLEV SCHOOL

Tempera on parchment
Size of sheet: height 35.5 cm; width 29 cm
Diameter of miniature 19 cm

On the frontispiece of every manuscript gospels, according to ancient traditions, was to be the image of the Evangelist, or his symbol. Among the eight
miniatures decorating the text of the "Morozov" Gospels the finest and the
most picturesque is one with an Angel, the symbol of St Matthew the Evangelist. The stalking figure of the Angel, if soaring in the air, is disposed
in a roundel, closing the composition and making the image complete and
calm. The light curvature of the outlines shows the original mastership of
the Rublev School. Delicate shades of light-blue and violet, soft interplay
of lights and darks stress the gentle figure of the Angel. The design on the
frame in the shape of trefoliate flowers disposed along the roundel at equal
distances and joined together by a thin line, originates from the Byzantine
manuscripts of the 10th-11th century.
The composition with St John the Evangelist dictating to Prochorus is
simple and logical. It is made in the traditions of the Rublev School. The
colouring of the miniature is performed in soft light-blue, greenish, violet,
golden-brown and reddish-pink shades. The background, nimbi, decorations and ornamentation of seats and pedestals are golden. The colours of the
composition suit very well together.
The miniatures of the "Morozov" Gospels are almost replicas, similar to the
miniatures of the "Khitrovo" Gospels kept at the present time in the State
Lenin Library. It is supposed that the miniatures of the "Khitrovo" Gospels
were painted by Andrei Rublev (c. 1370-1430) himself.

33. PUCHEZHA SHROUD OF CHRIST. 1441. NOVGOROD

Russian icon embroidery
Taffeta, coloured silks, golden and silver thread
Width 175 cm; width 225 (with border)
Came from Puchezha, Ivanovo Region, in 1930
Contributed by the Archbishop Euthymus of Novgorod (1434-58)

This shroud was made to order of the Archbishop Euthymus of Novgorod. The composition is surrounded by the suitable inscription embroidered in golden thread. Its name was derived from the town of Puchezha (Ivanovo Region) where it was discovered in 1930. The Puchezha shroud of Christ is the earliest relic of Russian icon embroidery.
The strict laconic composition of "The Entombment" is symmetrical and calm. An artist made the design on crimson taffeta, adhering to the icon-painting traditions of the Novgorodian School, at the early 15th century, put to use all the essential qualities of the material: he softened lines and colour. A milliner had chosen the colours of silk very carefully and used the technique of embroidery with a such artistic taste, that the Puchezha shroud may be numbered among the best masterpieces of the Russian and world embroidery.
Such shrouds were used in the Russian Orthodox Church to be spread over the Holy Sepulchre.

34,35. SHROUD "ST DEMETRIUS OF THESSALONICA". 15TH CENTURY

Russian icon embroidery
Taffeta, coloured silks, gold thread. Embroidery
Length 33.5 cm; width (with framing) 27 cm
Came from the Pushkin Museum of Fine Arts on April 15, 1927

The shroud adorned with the image of the saint warrior Demetrius of Thessalonica belongs to the earliest relics of the Russian icon embroidery kept in the Armoury. St Demetrius is embroidered on crimson taffeta in yellow, blue and flesh-coloured silks. The embroidery imitates icon-painting of the period. Just as on paintings, the composition is modest, even strict, colours are clear and bright. An artist stressed volumetrical rhythmical lines of the design; a milliner retained those lines, embroidering them in pink.

BYZANTINE ART OF 5TH-15TH CENTURIES

36,37. HELMET WITH "THE DEESIS". 13TH CENTURY. BYZANTIUM

Iron. Silver and gold damascening
Height (without top) 30 cm; diameter 23.5 cm; weight 2.25 kg
From the basic collection. Indexed in 1685
Former property of Ivan III Vassilievich (1440-1505), the Grand Prince of Moscow.
Brought to Moscow by the Greek Princess Sophia Paleologos, his second wife

The helmet has a broad vertical crown and a pointed top, hexagonal in the lower part and cone-shaped upwards; its form resembles that of a cap. A high spire is lost; holes at the top show where it was fixed. The helmet is ornamented with silver and gold damascening. The crown at the front bears the Deesis Range, and there are three saints at the back.
The iconography of the helmet dates from the reign of Paleologos dynasty.

38,39,40,41. EWER. C.400 A.D. CONSTANTINOPLE, BYZANTIUM

Silver, partly gilded. Chasing, carving, "kanfarenye"
Height 38.5 cm; weight 2.250 kg
Acquired in 1928
The ewer originates from the so-called "Sudzhensky treasure", discovered in 1918 at the upper reaches of the Sudzha River, Kursk region, near the village of Bolshoi Kamenets

The ewer has a narrow neck (the upper part of it is broken off) and is divided from the vessel's body with a protuberant clear-cut cylinder, under which on the neck of the ewer are embossed scrolls of a clinging vine in loose knots. On the broad middle part of the ewer the embossing in high relief shows nine Muses, the inspirers of art and sciences, with those objects that were appropriated to them, and their names inscribed in Greek. Scrolls of the acanthus leaves are embossed on the lower part of the vessel with half-figures of animals. A rectangular control stamp on the flat bottom has the picture of Tyche in a seated posture, symbolizing Constantinople. The style of this control stamp allows to date the vessel A.D.400, as being made on one of the Constantinople workshops.
The Muses are disposed at will on the middle band of the ewer: here there are Terpsichore, the Muse of dancing, with a cithara, Melpomene, the Muse

of tragedy, and Thalia, the Muse of comedy, with tragical and comical masks. On the other side of the ewer are the images of Calliope, the Muse of epos, with a scroll, and Urania, the Muse of astronomy, with a globe. The images, worked in *repoussé*, are clearly seen on the richly gilded background. The gilding was made through fire which shifted the gilded surfaces from the outlines of the ewer.

42. ICON "CHRIST BLESSING"
10TH CENTURY CAMEO. BYZANTIUM
15TH CENTURY SETTING. RUSSIA

Heliotrope, gold, gems. Carving, chasing
Height 12 cm; width 8.2 cm. Cameo: height 8.8 cm; width 5 cm
Came from the Annunciation Cathedral in the Moscow Kremlin in 1922

The head of Christ is bordered with a deeply cut-in inscription. There was a time when the eyes of Christ were inlaid with silver dots that are lost now. The rectangular cameo with the rounded top is put in a setting (supposed to be from a later, non-Byzantine, time), which is adorned with emeralds, garnets and agates. The verso of the setting is plain; in the lower part there is an inscription in Russian (perhaps, of the 17th century) indicating its weight.
The similar cameo is kept in the Victoria and Albert Museum, London

43. ICON "CHRIST BLESSING"
10TH CENTURY CAMEO. BYZANTIUM
15TH CENTURY SETTING. RUSSIA

Lapis-lazuli, gold. Carving, chasing
Height 15 cm; width 7.8 cm. Cameo: height 8,8 cm; width 5 cm
Came from the Annunciation Cathedral in the Moscow Kremlin in 1922

Christ is carved in high relief, at full length, the gospels in His left hand, His right raised for blessing. The nimbus and the book-cover are encrusted in golden dots.
The golden setting is of the later period. The upper part of it has the form of the fancy "kokoshnik" with a roundel containing a double eagle. A cross with four rounded ends is carved on the verso of the stone. Around the cross there is the following inscription: *"IC, XC/NUKA".*

44. SMALL ICON "THE CRUCIFIXION WITH INTERCEDING SAINTS". 11TH CENTURY. BYZANTIUM
SETTING. KIEVAN RUS. 12TH-13TH CENTURY

Gold, gems. Cloisonné enamel, filigree
Height 6.4 cm; width 5 cm
Discovered in 1822 in Staraya Ryazan, in the so-called "Staro-Ryazan Treasure"

The sacred image "The Crucifixion with Interceding Saints" is a perfect specimen of glorified *cloisonné* enamel of the 11th century when the culture of Byzantium was flourishing This sacred image is remarkable for its exquisite mastership, modest and clear-cut composition.
The obverse is ornamented with "The Crucifixion with Interceding Saints" that may be often seen on icons, sacred images and other common relics of Byzantine applied arts. Though the images of the saints are very small, they are expressive and stately. Under the cross there are skull and bones. Above, in the corners, there are half-figures of flying angels; at the very top there are sings meaning "the Sun and the Moon". The gold plate in *cloisonné* enamel is framed with an oval setting with a rich filigree ornament, adorned with granulation, and with twelve "nests" settings for precious stones; in three of them there are pearls.

45. SMALL ICON "THE DESCENT INTO HELL".12TH CENTURY.BYZANTIUM

Gold, silver. Cloisonné enamel, chasing niello
Height 9.5 cm; width 8.5 cm
Came from the Annunciation Cathedral in the Moscow Kremlin in 1922

The icon is rectangular; the gold verso is decorated with the complicated composition "The Descent into Hell" made in *cloisonné* enamel. Smothering the gate of Hell, Christ is leading Adam with His right hand, holding a six-pointed cross in His left. Right to Christ, behind Adam, stand Eve and Abel; left to Christ stand St John the Baptist, the King Constantine and the Queen Helen. The icon is in a silver setting with an ornamental border, also in *cloisonné* enamel.
The enamel is generally made in light-blue, green and red. The faces are made in pink enamel.

The reverse side bears a silver plaque with a Greek inscription in niello, referring to some relic or relics, and with a later incised inscription in Russian telling of the weight of the icon.

46. PHILOTHEUS' STAUROTHEQUE. 12TH CENTURY. BYZANTIUM

Gilded silver, wood. Chasing, carving
Height 20.5 cm; width 17 cm
From the basic collection
Tradition names the Patriarch Philotheus as the owner of the reliquary;brought to the Grand Prince Ivan Ivanovich in 1354 from Constantinople by the Metropolitan Alexius who had been consecrated there the Metropolitan

The staurothèque (a container for a cross) is rectangular; it has the form of a wooden box with traces of a sliding lid (now missing) and a cruciform recess with leavings of the wood said to be taken from Christ's Cross. The decoration consists of *repoussé* silver gilt plaques; the silver field is filled with ornamental plant design; on either side of the cruciform recess, under the lower traverse, there are full-length figures of St Cosmus on the left, and St Damyan on the right. Above there are two busts in medallions: St Cyrus, on the left, and St Panteleimon, on the right. The staurothèque is decorated with these saints having the power to cure diseases: SS Cosmus and Damyan are often pictured as doctors-healers. The same gift was attributed to St Panteleimon. St Cyrus, as the legend said, was the doctor from Alexandria. On three parts of the frame there is an inscription in Greek bordered with a twisted band imitating filigree. The lateral sides of the frame are decorated with *repoussé* ornamentation.

47. ICON "ST DEMETRIUS OF THESSALONICA"
11TH CENTURY BAS-RELIEF.
14TH CENTURY FRAME. BYZANTIUM

Steatite, silver. Carving, chasing
Height 31.4 cm; width 26.4 cm. Bas-relief: height 11.8 cm, width 9.7 cm
Came from the Museum of Porcelain in 1926
As the legend said, the icon was presented to the Grand Prince of Moscow Dmitri Donskoi (1350-89) by a Byzantine Emperor as memento and benediction in connection with the victory at the Kulikovo Field in 1380

The image of St Demetrius of Thessalonica on horseback is carved on a steatite plaque. He was considered to be the inspirer of warriors in Byzantium and Russia both. The silver frame of the icon is decorated with a plant ornament, the busts of Christ and the Archangels Michael and Gabriel (above), three saint warriors, SS Mercurius, Nicetas and Arthemius (below). This unusual combination of the Archangels and warriors prove that the production of this icon was really connected with the struggle of Dmitri Donskoi against the Tartars.
The plaques with SS Basil and John Chrysostom at full length were added later and most probably refer to the Grand Princes of Moscow by the same name.

48. ICON "THE VIRGIN ENTHRONED"
12TH CENTURY CAMEO. BYZANTIUM
15TH CENTURY SETTING. NOVGOROD

Lapis-lazuli, gilded silver, gems, pearls. Carving, filigree, chasing
Height 11.5 cm; width 7,8 cm. Cameo: height 7 cm; width 5.5 cm
Came from the Annunciation Cathedral in the Moscow Kremlin in 1922
One side of the frame is ornamented with a following inscription: "This icon was made by order of the Archbishop Euthymus of Novgorod the Great"

The cameo displays the Virgin Enthroned, made in low relief, her head slightly turned towards the Child seated on her left hand. The throne and the garments of Mary are covered with hollowed cut patterns for inlaid decoration. The crown and the clothes are covered with small dots where silver disseminations used to be. The cameo is framed with the filigree setting of gilded silver made in Novgorod in the 15th century. The reverse side of the setting is adorned with the carved images of SS Euthymus and John the Evangelist at full length.

49,50. ICON "ST JOHN THE FORERUNNER". 14TH CENTURY. BYZANTIUM OBVERSE AND VERSO

Steatite, gilded silver. Carving, chasing
Height 12.3 cm; width 6.5 cm. Relief: height 12 cm; width 6.2 cm
Came from the Annunciation Cathedral in the Moscow Kremlin in 1922

The steatite plaque with St John the Forerunner is enclosed into a silver gilded setting. The verso of it is adorned with the carved hatching of a

four-pointed cross in the centre; below the cross is the Greek-Latin control stamp. On the sides are monograms with letters "A" (the beginning) and "Ω" (the end); above, there are the Sun and the Moon.

51. "PHOTIUS" MOUNTING OF ICON "THE VIRGIN OF VLADIMIR". EARLY 15TH CENTURY. DETAIL. BYZANTIUM

Gold. Filigree, chasing
Mounting: height 150 cm; width 70 cm
Came from the Dormition Cathedral in the Moscow Kremlin

The gold mounting, called "the Photius", was most probably made by Greek masters for the icon "The Virgin of Vladimir" which had been particularly revered in Russia, and was kept at the period in the Dormition Cathedral in the Moscow Kremlin. The mounting was made to order of the Archbishop Photius who was ordained the Metropolitan of Moscow in 1409.
The borders of the mounting are decorated with the Twelve Church Feasts made in *repoussé* on rectangular gold plaques. The contour presents a plant ornament made of fine strips of metal welded edgewise on the surface. The filigree pattern represents a neverending winding branch with many curling sprouts, flowers and leaves, and among them we find circles, stars, lozenges and crosses sprouting flowers. A similar design may be often found on Byzantine craftsmanship. This design reminds filigree ornament of the Monomachos Cap of State, or of the "Morozov" Gospels.
The *repoussé* plaques with the Church Feasts on the mounting (one of them, "The Entry into Jerusalem", is presented here) are distinguished for their high technique, though the art of Byzantium in the 15th century was following into decay which comes out strongly in the crude tedious composition.

52, 53, 54. SHRINE. 11TH CENTURY. BYZANTIUM

Silver with traces of gilding. Chasing
Height 16 cm; width 11.5 cm
Came from the Patriarch Vestry in 1920
Supposed to be made to order of the State Secretary John Autorianus in 1059-69

The shrine reproduces a tabernacle over the grave of St Demetrius of Thessalonica in Salonica.
Each arch has a silver chalice symbolizing a lamp which was usually put together with a candle on the top of the sarcophagus. The shrine is octagonal; some sides are broad, others narrow. One of the broad sides represents a door with mobile folds, ornamented with *repoussé* images of SS Nestor and Lupus, as the "custodians" at the portal of the sarcophagus. Upon another we find the Emperor couple blessed by Christ: they are the Byzantine Emperor Constantine XI Ducas (1059-67), and his spouse Eudoxie, the daughter of Constantine Dalassina. Such representation ranked the Imperial family equal to homage and meant legal power and the infallibility of the rulers. The policy of Constantine XI at home strove for a supreme power at time of complete victory of feudalism in Byzantium. One more side of the shrine is ornamented with a *repoussé* Greek inscription, the dedication. The narrow sides are decorated with large stylized plant ornament, typical for Byzantine ornamentation.

55. SAKKOS OF METROPOLITAN PETER OF MOSCOW. 1322

Byzantine fabric
Ornamentation in pearls of Russian work
Brocaded satin, damask, gilded silver, pearls. Hand-weaving, chasing, filigree, gilding
Length 137 cm; width (with sleeves) 142 cm
Came from the Patriarch Vestry in 1920

The sakkos of the first Moscow Metropolitan Peter belongs to the most ancient specimen of tissues kept in the Armoury at the present time. These original and noble tissues with a "crescent" pattern were used only for ecclesiastical robes of high priesthood. Such robes symbolized high dignity of their possessors. Images of the saints wearing the "crescent" robes could be seen in embroidery, fresco and easel painting, small castings and carvings, etc. The Metropolitan Peter is portrayed in this sakkos on a hearsecloth of 1519, the same on an ivory icon of the 15th century, kept both in the Armoury, as well as on an icon of the Dormition Cathedral in the Moscow Kremlin, made by the great Russian artist Dionysius
The yoke and the sleeves of the sakkos were embroidered with silver gilded orphreys and fine river pearls in the 14th century, to which were added later new orphreys instead the lost ones.

56, 57. "MAJOR" SAKKOS OF METROPOLITAN PHOTIUS OF MOSCOW

Byzantine icon embroidery. 1414-17
Ornamentation in pearls of Russian work. 15th century

Satin, wire-drawn gold and silver, coloured silks, pearls
Length 135 cm; width 112 cm (with sleeves)
Came from the Patriarch Vestry in 1920
Sent by Manuel 11 (1391-1425), Emperor of Byzantium, to the Grand Prince of Moscow
Vassili Dmitrievich (1371-1425), son of Dmitri Donskoi

The sakkos is made of blue satin embroidered with gold and silver thread, as well as with coloured silkes; it is decorated with many compositions (more than one thousand): scenes from the gospels, images of the saints, the Metropolitan Photius (1409-31) himself, portraits of the Grand Prince of Moscow Vassili Dmitrievich, his wife Sophia Witowtovna, their daughter Anna and her husband John Paleologos, future Emperor of Byzantium, with accompanying inscriptions. Near the images of the Grand Prince Vassili and the Grand Princess Sophia there are inscriptions in Russian. This work is to prove the growing power and authority of the Grand Prince of Moscow whose support the Emperor of Byzantium was eager to secure during difficulties of his reign. In the 12th century wire-drawn gold in Byzantium was replaced in embroidery with cheaper gold thread, so the use of wire-drawn gold for this sakkos shows the extraordinary importance which had been attached to it in Constantinople.
Later, in the 16th-17th century, the sakkos had been worn on special ceremonies. For example, it was used by the Patriarch Joachim at the coronation of the Russian tsars, the brothers Ivan Alexeevich and Peter Alexeevich (later Peter the Great) in 1682.

58, 59. "MINOR" SAKKOS OF METROPOLITAN PHOTIUS OF MOSCOW. MID-14TH CENTURY

Byzantine icon embroidery
Satin, wire-drawn gold and silver, coloured silks, pearls
Length 142.0 cm; width (with sleeves) 150.0 cm
Came from the Patriarch Vestry in 1920

The "Minor" sakkos of the Metropolitan Photius (1409-31) was made in Constantinople in the mid-14th century of which the simple and laconic embroidery indicates. The Metropolitan Peter of Moscow (1308-26) presented among Greek saints also tells of the earlier production of the sakkos. Obviously, it was sent to Moscow in connection with the canonization of the Metropolitan Peter in 1339. The image of the Metropolitan Peter is placed in the vertical row, right from the central composition, in the third arch from the top.
The dark-blue satin background is embroidered with wire-drawn gold and silver with images of saints, scenes of the Church Feasts, and the text of the "Symbol of Faith". Though the prevailing quantity of gold and silver in the work, the embroidery is extraordinary picturesque, because of many-coloured silks. In colour and scenery the sakkos resembles the best masterpieces of contemporary painting of that time.
Upon the cross, inside the round encircling the centre, is embroidered "The Crucifixion with Interceding Saints": the Virgin, Mary Magdalene, John the Theologian and Login Sotnik. Around the cross there are the prophets: Isaiah, Jeremiah, Micah and Sophonius, at full length, holding unrolled scrolls
The body of Christ and the faces of the saints are embroidered with pale silk, while the clothes, nimbi and the field are embroidered with wire-drawn gold and silver.

RUSSIAN ART OF 16TH CENTURY

60, 61. "BAIDANA" OF TSAR BORIS GODUNOV. 16TH CENTURY. MADE BY MOSCOW CRAFTSMEN

Iron. Forging, chasing
Length 80 cm; width of shoulders 65 cm; weight 6.250 kg. Ring: 0.24 cm; width of surface 0.05 cm
From the basic collection. Indexed in 1598 in the Inventory of the Tsar Boris Godunov's property

The word "baidana" originates from the Arabian "badan" which means a short armour made of large flat interlinked rings of *repoussé* iron. "Baidana" is an original variety of the coat of mail. The wide surfaces of the rings were decorated with ornaments and inscriptions. On every ring of the "baidana" there is a stamped inscription: "God is with us, nobody will touch us". The similar inscriptions often decorated Russian armours and military standards in particular up to World War I.
The "baidana" consists of more than ten thousand rings. The Inventory of 1598 mentioned that the hem of the "baidana" was ornamented with three rows of copper gilded rings, while the front was decorated with three big targets of gilded copper.

62   BATTLE-AXES AND BATTLE-PICKS. 16TH CENTURY
From left to right

"TOPOROK" (SMALL BATTLE-AXE). MADE BY MOSCOW CRAFTSMEN

Steel, iron, gold, mahogany. Forging, damascening
Length from back to edge 15 cm; length with hilt 66.5 cm; total weight 0.920 kg
From the basic collection. Indexed in 1685

"KLEVETS" (BATTLE-PICK). MADE BY ARMOURY CRAFTSMEN

Steel, iron, copper, walnut, "khoz" leather. Forging, damascening
Length of battle-pick 22 cm; length with hilt 78.5 cm; total weight 0.880 kg
From the basic collection. Indexed in 1685

BATTLE-AXE. TURKEY

Steel, silver, wood, "khoz" leather. Forging, niello
Length from back to edge 14 cm; length with hilt 69 cm; total weight 0.740 kg
From the basic collection. Indexed in 1685

BATTLE-AXE. BOKHARA

Steel, wood, silver. Forging, damascening
Length from back to edge 15 cm; length with hilt 60 cm
From the basic collection. Indexed in 1685

"KLEVETS" (BATTLE-PICK). KUBAN. RUSSIA

Steel, silver, wood, leather
Length 27 cm; length with hilt 77.5 cm; total weight 1.130 kg
From the basic collection

Battle-axes, battle-picks and battle-hammers ("chekans") were side-arms intended to strike hard the enemy from the helm. The weapon was to break metal plates and rings of the link-woven defensive armour.

63. STANDARD OF YERMAK TIMOFEEVICH. 1581-2

Water-colour on canvas
Length 200 cm; width 150 cm
This standard was brought in the Armoury in 1834 from Tobolsk by the Commander of the Tobolsk artillery garrison, the second lieutenant Shirokovsky with the report that "this standard was with Yermak Timofeevich when he conquered Siberia, under the Tsar Ivan Vassilievich in 1582".

In the centre of the standard are images of the Archangel Michael and Joshua kneeling by the walls of the biblical city of Jericho. The central part of the standard is bordered with brown canvas where in water-colours are painted rich stylized flowers, with big rosettes in the corners Above there is the inscription: "Formidable Voivode Archangel Michael". The Archangel Michael was considered to be the patron saint of the Russian army.
The mentioned standard is one of the three kept in the Armoury. The other two of blue canvas are decorated with "lion and unicorn ready to fight"...—so the old documents tell.

64. DISH OF TSARINA MARIA TEMRYUKOVNA. 1561. MADE IN WORKSHOPS OF MOSCOW KREMLIN

Gold, niello, chasing, forging, carving
Diameter 42 cm; weight 4.987 kg
Came from the State Museum in Zagorsk in 1928
Made for wedding day of the Tsar Ivan the Terrible(1530-84) and Circassian Princess Maria Temryukovna, on August 21, 1561. The dish was presented by the Tsar to his young wife

This solid dish, ornamented in niello, is hammered from a gold leaf weighing about three kilogrammes. Its bottom is worked in *repoussé* with spoon-shaped depressions, strongly curved and radiating from the circle with a double eagle The brim of the dish is ornamented in niello. Among the plant design, painted by a skilful and easy hand, there are scroll-shaped control-stamps with an inscription referring to the origin of the dish made for wedding day of Ivan the Terrible.
According to wedding rites of early Russia, the bride's head-dress, "kika", was presented up on such a gold dish. The simple, clear-cut form, gentle outlines giving the interplay of lights and shades, mat twinkling of gold (due to long and scrupulous forging), the beautiful and noble design in niello make it possible to call the dish a classical masterpiece of decorative applied art. Up to the late 17th century this dish attached attention of jewellers. Several similar dished were made again in the 17th century, but not the single could compete with the dish of Maria Temryukovna in perfect craftsmanship and beauty.

65. GOSPELS OF TSAR IVAN THE TERRIBLE. COVER. 1568. MADE IN WORKSHOPS OF MOSCOW KREMLIN

Gilded silver, velvet. Chasing, filigree, carving, casting, granulation
Height 33.5 cm; width 21 cm
The chancel Gospels in the silver cover were made in 1568 to order of Ivan the Terrible
(1530-84); later contributed by him into the Annunciation Cathedral in the Moscow
Kremlin

The background of the central portion of the cover is ornamented with an open-worked filigree pattern, fine and clear-cut, made of wires flattened out. Among the filigree design and on the borders of the cover, in deepened keel-like icon-cases, are disposed cast figures of saints, soldered on the background.
The very border of the cover is ornamented with a presentation inscription and a wide frame separated from the central part of the cover by a row of small pyramids of granulation; the frame is adorned with twenty cast images of the Old Testament Trinity, busts of the Archangels and of the saints disposed in the three keel-like laciniate arches.
Soft lines of the figures of the saints are calm and noble. Their elongated proportions, as well as the elongated cover, give the impression of peaceful solemnity.
The Gospels were made upon the model of the Gospels of 1392 belonged to the Boyard Feodor Koshka; now they are kept in the State Lenin Library.

66. PANAGIA OF PATRIARCH JOB
1589 SETTING. MADE IN WORKSHOPS OF MOSCOW KREMLIN
12TH CENTURY CAMEO. BYZANTIUM

Agate, gold, gems, pearls. Enamel, niello, filigree, granulation, chasing, carving
Height 15.8 cm; width 8.8 cm. Cameo: height 6 cm; width 6 cm
Came from the Patriarch Vestry in 1919
Presented by the Tsar Feodor Ivanovich and the Tsarina Irina to the first Patriarch of
Moscow and All Russia Job (1589-1605) in the day of his elevation to the rank, on
February 28, 1589

The centre of the panagia is decorated with the Byzantine cameo of the 12th century made of double-layered agate with the carved picture of "The Crucifixion with Interceding Saints" on the face, and images of SS Constantine and Helen on the reverse side.
The setting of the panagia is adorned with the finest filigree ornament filled with bright delicate enamel. Gems are disposed among the filigree pattern. The reverse side of the setting is plain but for a long presentation inscription.

67. CHANCEL CROSS. 1562. MADE IN WORKSHOPS OF MOSCOW KREMLIN

Gold, gems, pearls. Enamel, niello, filigree, carving, chasing, forging
Height 40 cm; width of middle cross-beam 19 cm
Came from the Museum Fund in 1922
Made by craftsmen of the Moscow Kremlin to order of the Tsar Ivan the Terrible and
contributed by him into the Solovetsky Monastery in 1562 "for the health of the Tsare-
vichs Ivan and Feodor"

The cross is one of the numerous and rich gifts by the Tsar Ivan the Terrible to the far off Solovetsky Monastery founded in the mid-15th century on an island in the White Sea.
The background of the obverse is covered with a very fine plant ornament which was typical to Moscow art of the period. Filigree is run with many-coloured enamel, the colours of white, light-blue and green dominating. Among the ornamentations there are placed gems.
The reverse side is decorated with the carved inscription referring to the contribution of the cross.

68. "MERNAYA" ICON "ST JOHN CLIMACUS" IN MOUNTING. 1554. MADE IN WORKSHOPS OF MOSCOW KREMLIN

Tempera on wood. Gold, gems, pearls. Enamel, chasing
Height 46 cm; width 17.2 cm
Came from the Archangel Michael Cathedral in the Moscow Kremlin in 1922

"Mernaya" ("measured") was the name given to the narrow long icons on wood, the length of which was that of a new-born baby in the royal family. Such icons were decorated with an image of a saint whose name was given to a tsarevich. Here is the image of St John Climacus whose name was given to the second son of Ivan the Terrible, born on March 28, 1554.
The gold background of the middle part of the mounting, as well as the framing, are covered with a filigree ornament run with white, blue, light-blue and green enamel. The exquisite filigree pattern is in harmony with

gentle enamelled flowers. The slightest drops of golden granulation "sprayed" by the master all over the design, crown the masterpiece. The magnificent mounting suits to the style of painting performed in the best traditions of the Tsar's icon-painting workshop.

69. CENSER OF TSARINA IRINA. 1598. MADE IN WORKSHOPS OF MOSCOW KREMLIN

Gold, gems, chasing, granulation, carving, "kanfarenye"
Height 29 cm; width of side 10.3 cm
Came from the Archangel Michael Cathedral in the Moscow Kremlin in 1919
Contributed by the Tsarina Irina into the Archangel Michael Cathedral in the Moscow
Kremlin

The golden censer of the Tsarina Irina is remarkable for its exceptional beauty and artistic work. It reproduces a cubical temple with an onion-like dome, cut windows on the drum, and the floor with two rows of ornamentation in ogee arch style, which was typical for Moscow architecture of the period. The dome, the "kokoshniks" and the base of the censer are decorated with the fine nielloed grasses, sprouts and flowers. Three sides of the censer are adorned with nielloed images of the elongated slim figures of the Apostles. Their faces are so expressive, their movements so graceful and natural, that they seem to have been sketched with a pen. The fourth side of the censer is ornamented with the images of the saints, the patrons of the royal family.
The censer was so much estimated for its beauty that it was used only on special occasions, and no often than nine times a year. It was recorded in the Patriarch Act at the early 17th century.

70. CHALICE OF TSARINA IRINA. 1598. MADE IN WORKSHOPS OF MOSCOW KREMLIN

Gold, gems. Chasing, niello, carving
Height 27 cm; diameter of bowl 14 cm
Came from the Archangel Michael Cathedral in the Moscow Kremlin in 1919
Contributed by the Tsarina Irina into the Archangel Michael Cathedral after the death
of her husband, the Tsar Feodor Ivanovich (1557-98) in 1598

A carved inscription on spoon-like depressions of the chalice stand tells about the production of the cup. The chalice is extraordinary beautiful and harmonious; the exquisite and noble decoration competes with its shape on the whole. The broad polished crown is somewhat simple and is made deliberately modest. Contrasting with the crown, the surface of the bowl is covered with large nielloed design among which there are the medallions with winged seraphim and big gems in high casts.

71. ICON "CHRIST ALMIGHTY" IN MOUNTING. SECOND HALF
16TH CENTURY

Tempera on wood. Gilded silver, gems, pearls. Chasing, carving, "kanfarenye"
Height 50 cm; width 40.5 cm
Came from the Pokrovsky Nunnery in Suzdal in 1931
Contributed by a member of Ivan the Terrible family

The design and colouring of the mounting are entirely in harmony with the picture itself. The red tunic of Christ, ornamented with gold, and His greenish-blue himation are rendered brightest because of blue sapphires and crimson almandines in high "nest" settings, symmetrically placed on the crown, crescent collars and the wide frame of the silver mounting. The ornamentation embossed in high relief on the frame is remarkable for its gorgeous design and mastership; the design is formed by a spiral stalk winding in different directions, in the curves of which gems are found; where two stalks join there are oval orphreys with carved figures of the saints. Their svelte figures are characteristic for 16th century Russian art. The general outlines of the composition are stressed with large pearls. The ornamentation in *repoussé* on the borders of the mounting, in the shape of leaved pomegranates flattened out, resembles the stylized control stamps of the Oriental type.

72. GOSPELS OF TSAR IVAN THE TERRIBLE. COVER. 1571. MADE IN WORKSHOPS OF MOSCOW KREMLIN

Gold, gems, pearls. Enamel, filigree, granulation, niello, chasing, carving
Height 42.5 cm; width 30 cm
Came from the Annunciation Cathedral in the Moscow Kremlin in 1919
Made by craftsmen of the Moscow Kremlin to order of the Tsar Ivan the Terrible.
Contributed by the Tsar Ivan the Terrible into the Annunciation Cathedral in the
Moscow Kremlin in 1571

The chancel Gospels are in a golden cover. The nielloed inscription on the plain narrow frame, which borders the central part of the cover, says about the origin of the Gospels.

The front of the cover is decorated with fine filigree plant ornament; the fine flowers and petals in enamel are of light gentle shades. The filigree of the cover is soldered on at a certain angle to make the design vivid and graceful. The granulation, in the shape of the slightest golden drops, or diminitive vine grapes, adds splendour to it. The colour range of the cover in gold and enamel is rendered more conspicuous by jewels, sapphires in particular, favourite gem in the 16th century. In the centre of the cover there is the traditional composition "The Descent into Hell"; at corners there are placed the symbols of the Evangelists. The narrow bands with words of prayers in niello border the medallions and gems.

The Gospels belong to the best masterpieces of decorative applied art of the 16th century. The jewellers have used all kinds of handiwork in an excellent and artistic way.

73. SADDLE OF TSAR BORIS GODUNOV. SECOND HALF 16TH CENTURY. MADE BY CRAFTSMEN OF CAVALRY OFFICE

Wood, velvet, gold, gems. Hand-weaving, embroidery, casting, chasing
Came from the Cavalry Office between 1720-36

"POKROVETS" (SMALL HORSE-CLOTH). MID-17TH CENTURY. MADE BY CRAFTSMEN OF CAVALRY OFFICE

Satin, wire-drawn gold, gold thread, looped glass. Hand-weaving
Length 141 cm; width 179 cm
Came from the Cavalry Office between 1720-36

The shape of this saddle is typical for Russian saddles of the 16th century; it has a special construction which gave a rider a possibility to stir freely when on horseback. The saddle was put on the horse by means of saddle berths. The pommel was tall and wide, the rear arch low and sloping. The saddle for a well-bred horse usually was richtly decorated. Some portions of ornamentation are trimmed with gold in such a way that the pattern becomes more convex.

74. SAKKOS OF METROPOLITAN DIONYSIUS OF MOSCOW. LATE 16TH CENTURY. MADE IN TSARINA'S WORKSHOP

Iranien fabric
Satin brocaded, pearls, gold. Hand-weaving, niello, enamel
Length 135 cm; width of shoulders 142 cm
Came from the Patriarch Vestry in 1920
Contributed by the Tsar Ivan the Terrible into the Dormition Cathedral in the Moscow Kremlin in 1583, in memory of his killed son, Tsarevich Ivan Ivanovich

The fabric of the sakkos belongs to the rarest kind of the Oriental satins of the 16th century, where elements of late-Byzantine style (images of the Virgin, angels and crosses) are interlaced with Iranian plant ornamentation. It is possible that this fabric was specially made in the court workshops of the Shah Abbas I (1557—1628) to be exported into Russia.

Borders of the sakkos are embroidered with pearls and gold orphreys in niello and enamel. The pattern of the embroidery is adopted from Russian folk art. The fine and clear-cut design, variously modifying the principal theme, is a proof to the creative work of the milliners at Tsarina's workshop. Exquisite and noble embroidery is in harmony with the splendour of the fabric. The pattern is distinguished for a certain finish in the embroideries.

75. SAKKOS OF METROPOLITAN ANTHONY. SLEEVES. LATE 16TH CENTURY

Ornamentation in pearls of Russian work
Damask, gilded silver, pearls, gold thread. Chasing, gilding
Height 21 cm; length 63 cm
Came from the Patriarch Vestry in 1920

The sleeves of the sakkos of the Metropolitan Anthony (1572-81) is a typical specimen of Russian embroidery in the 16th century. The regular arrangement in the structure of the whole pattern is created by large keel-shaped orphreys made of gilded silver, with the *repoussé* images of saints at half-length. The orphreys are bordered with pearls of middle size and contained into adjacent frames, formed by pearl plant sprouts. The edges of the sleeves are decorated with a row of small plain plates in the form of a circle, or a trapecium also bordered with pearls.

The composition is rendered intelligible and appealing by soft interplay of the light-blue field with the gentle gilding of orphreys and opaque shimmering of pearls.

76. PHELONION. EARLY 17TH CENTURY. MADE IN TSARINA'S WORKSHOP

Ornamentation in pearls of Russian work
Turkish fabric
Brocaded satin, velvet, gold, pearls, gems. Hand-weaving
Length 153 cm
Came from the Patriarch Vestry in 1920
Contributed by the Tsar Boris Godunov into the Archangel Michael Cathedral in the Moscow Kremlin in 1602 in memory of the Tsar Feodor Ivanovich

The design and colour of the phelonion are typical for Turkish art of the late 16th—early 17th century. The cost of the fabric depended on the size of the design: the larger the design, the more expensive the fabric. The patterns were intended for the wide cut of Oriental clothes. Vestments of high priesthood had the straight cut, so the Oriental fabrics suited this purpose very well.

The yoke of the phelonion is embroidered in the best traditions of Russian art. The pattern of the whole web passes from a rather complicated though imposing design into the fine embroidery of the yoke. Yet the Russian elements take advantage over the Oriental. The most beautiful are gold orphreys with fine nielloed compositions stressed with black colour of the plain velvet field. On the narrow gold orphreys, framing the yoke, is the nielloed inscription referring to the production of the phelonion to order of the Tsar Boris Feodorovich.

77. CEREMENT. 1598. MADE IN TSARINA'S WORKSHOP

Russian portrait embroidery
Damask, gold and silver thread, coloured silk, pearls, gems
Length 52 cm; width 54.0 cm
Came from the Patriarch Vestry in 1920
Contributed by the Tsarina Irina into the Archangel Michael Cathedral in the Moscow Kremlin in memory of the Tsar Feodor Ivanovich in 1598

The cerement is made in style of the so-called Godunov School of embroidery. In the 16th-17th century such embroideries became exceedingly gorgeous, due to the materials and the high technique of its production. It was an imitation of jewelry; gold, pearls and gems were used in plenty.

The cerement is ornamented with the traditional ecclesiastic design: a Lamb on the paten under the "zvezdnitsa", and two flanking angels. At the sides of the paten there are embroidered the words in gold thread referring to the production of this chasuble. The embroidery in silk, gold and silver thread is trimmed with pearls. The colours of the cerement are very beautiful: red damask contrasts with a blue border, the mat glittering of pearls is supplemented with the brilliance of rubies, sapphires and emeralds

The inscription at the border ("Take, eat"...), made in complicated Slavonic characters, is framed with large pearls, making it luxurious and wealthy. The border could be qualified as a separate masterpiece of decorative art.

78. SAKKOS OF PATRIARCH NICON. 1654

Ornamentation in pearls of Russian work. Late 16th century
Italian fabric. 17th century
Double looped hexamite. Gold, gems, pearls. Hand-weaving, niello
Length 134 cm; width (with sleeves) 134 cm
Came from the Patriarch Vestry in 1920

The sakkos is made of double looped hexamite of Italian work, the most valuable and luxurious tissue in the 17th century.

The ornamentation of the sakkos formerly has adorned the sakkos of the Metropolitan Dionysius, made to order of Ivan the Terrible in 1583, in Tsarina's workshop. Every large orphrey in the shape of the icon-case is the excellent gold nielloed miniature with the traditional religious composition. These orphreys sewn on the hem make the sakkos conspicuous for its natural beauty. They are made in imitation the ancient bone-lace "ogorody". Quantity of pearls, gems and gold orphreys on the sakkos reaches 24 kg. The sakkos was worn only on special ceremonies. Thus, in 1752 it was taken out from the Patriarch Vestry where it has been kept since 1655.

RUSSIAN ART OF 17TH CENTURY

79, 80. "ZERTSALOS" OF TSAR ALEXEI MIKHAILOVICH. 1663. MADE BY NIKITA DAVYDOV

Steel, copper silk. Gilding, silvering, chasing
Length 75 cm; width of shoulders 55 cm; weight 12.300 kg

Nikita Davydov, the hereditary blacksmith from Murom, was invited to the Workshops of the Armoury as an armourer. He was indexed in lists of armourers since 1617, worked about fifty years. On June 24, 1664 he was let off to a monastery because of his old age. Date of his death is unknown.

The "zertsalos" consists of breast- and back-pieces, made of separate plaques. The breast-plate consists of 15 plaques and the necklace; the back-piece consists of 15 plaques, the necklace and two yokes The surface of every plaque is worked in *repoussé* with grooves in the shape of rafters. The grooves are inlaid alternately with gold and silver. All plaques are trimmed with a silver fringe. Under the plaques there is the quilted red silk lining. The cuirass was a defensive armour against side-arms and pricking weapons. After the introduction of fire-arms, the "zertsalos" little by little disappeared from the military complex of a warrior. The last "zertsalos" made to order of the Tsar Alexei Mikhailovich (1629-76) were produced by the armourers Grigori Viatkin and Vassili Titov in 1670.

81. "BAKHTERETS" OF TSAR MIKHAIL FEODOROVICH. 1620. MADE BY KONON MIKHAILOV (active first quarter 17th century)

Iron. Forging, chasing, gold damascening
Length 70 cm; width 60 cm; weight 12 kg
From the basic collection. Indexed in 1685

The defensive armour called "bakhterets", combined plate and mail, was made in the Armoury by Konon Mikhailov. Large rings at its front, back and sides were changed into the interlinked plaques. The armour consists of twelve rows of plaques, 1,200 in number. All the plaques are decorated with fine gold damascening. The lengthwise plaques are laid one on the other, from bottom to top. The "bakhterets" is done up with the silver clasps with fixed straps.
The armour was used in hand-to-hand fighting and perfectly protected a warrior from side-arms. The "bakhterets" was very popular among military leaders of Russian army.

82. SADDLE OF TSAR MIKHAIL FEODOROVICH. 1637-8. MADE BY IVAN POPOV AND COMPANIONS. SILVER HALL

Spanish fabric. 17th century
Wood, looped hexamite, gold, gems. Embroidery, enamel
From the basic collection

"CHALDAR" OF TSAR ALEXEI MIKHAILOVICH. SECOND HALF 17TH CENTURY. MADE BY CRAFTSMEN OF CAVALRY OFFICE

Italian fabric. 17th century
Silk, lace, gold and silver thread, "kandek", satin. Hand-weaving
Length 170 cm; width 180 cm
Came from the Cavalry Office between 1720-36

The horse-saddle of the Tsar Mikhail Feodorovich (1596-1645) was made, as it is recorded, by the best craftsmen of the Moscow Kremlin Ivan Popov and his companions. The saddle was intended for the parade horse of the Tsar and was richly decorated with gold and gems. According to the account books of that time, it says that on January 22, 1637 Vassili Ivanovich Streshnev has taken from the Royal Palace a gold chain weighing two pounds and ordered to trim the saddle with this gold.
The "chaldar" covered the breast and sides of the horse of the Tsar Alexei Mikhailovich (1645-76). The luxurious silver design on Italian silk is supplemented by Russian crescent silver lace, as well as the long fringe of the border.

83, 84. ARQUEBUSES. 17TH CENTURY. MADE BY CRAFTSMEN OF ARMOURY

MATCHLOCKS from left to right

BUTT-STOCKS from right to left

ARQUEBUS. MADE BY ANDRONOV. FIRST HALF 17TH CENTURY

Iron, wood, ivory. Chasing, gilding, encrustation
Total length 123.6 cm; total weight 3.812 kg; calibre 10 mm
From the basic collection. Indexed in 1685

ARQUEBUS. SECOND HALF 17TH CENTURY

Iron, wood, ivory. Chasing, gilding, encrustation
Total length 138.2 cm; total weight 3.930 kg; calibre 9 mm
From the basic collection. Indexed in 1685

ARQUEBUS. SECOND HALF 17TH CENTURY

Iron, wood, mother-of-pearl, ivory. Chasing, gilding, encrustation
Total length 135.4 cm; total weight 3. 650 kg; calibre 9 mm

ARQUEBUS OF PETER THE GREAT. 1692

Iron, wood, ivory. Chasing, gilding, encrustation
Total length 137.9 cm; total weight 4.140 kg; calibre 10 mm
From the basic collection
The barrel is damascened in gold: "The arquebus of the Tsar and the Grand Prince Peter Alexeevich, the ruler of All Russia, 1692".

ARQUEBUS. SECOND HALF 17TH CENTURY

Iron, wood, mother-of-pearl. Chasing, encrustation
Total length 132.7 cm; total weight 3.650 kg; calibre 13 mm
From the basic collection

ARQUEBUS

Iron, wood, ivory, mother-of-pearl. Chasing, encrustation
Total length 136.5 cm; total weight 3.350 kg; calibre 12 mm
From the basic collection

The arquebuses with flint locks were charged through the muzzle hole with a help of the ramrod. The cocking-pieces have shapes of various fantastic animals. The bores of the barrels have a spiral rifling from left to upwards, clockwise, as the modern rifles have.

85, 86. ARQUEBUSES. 17TH CENTURY. MADE BY CRAFTSMEN OF ARMOURY

MATCHLOCKS from left to right

BUTTS from right to left

ARQUEBUS. MADE BY OSIP ALFEEV. 1659-64

Iron, wood, mother-of-pearl. Gilding, silvering, encrustation
Total length 113.5 cm; total weight 2.480 kg; calibre 13 mm
From the basic collection. Indexed in 1685

ARQUEBUS. MADE BY VASSILI TITOV (died in 1681). 1650-80

Iron, wood, ivory; Chasing, gilding, encrustation
Total length 136.5 cm; total weight 4.595 kg; calibre 12 mm
From the basic collection. Indexed in 1685
The inscription on the barrel: "Made by Vassili Titov"

ARQUEBUS

Iron, wood, ebony, ivory. Chasing, gilding, encrustation
Total length 136.2 cm; total weight 2.480 kg; calibre 13 cm
From the basic collection. Indexed in 1685

ARQUEBUS

Iron, wood, ivory. Chasing, gilding, encrustation
Total length 138.8 cm; total weight 4.040 kg; calibre 12 cm
From the basic collection. Indexed in 1685

ARQUEBUS

Iron, wood, mother-of-pearl. Chasing, gilding, encrustation
Total length 128 cm; total weight 3.306 kg; calibre 10 mm
From the basic collection. Indexed in 1685

ARQUEBUS

Iron, wood, ivory. Chasing, gilding, encrustation
Total length 125 cm; total weight 1.370 kg; calibre 10 mm
From the basic collection. Indexed in 1685

Rich decorated fire-arms were very much in demand in the 17th century for the royal hunting. The fire-arms were ornamented with encrustation in ivory and mother-of-pearl, as well as with forging, gilding and silvering.
The decorations of the butt-stocks were made by the masters of the Armoury: Vassili Kartsov, Evtikhi Kuzovlev, Larion Dimitriev and Mikhail Chernorudny.

87. COLOURS ("PRAPOR") OF VLADIMIR REGIMENTS OF RUSSIAN ARMY. 17TH CENTURY

Silk. Colour painting
Length 250 cm; width 80 cm
From the basic collection

In the centre of the colour, surrounded by a wreath, is the coat of arms of the town of Vladimir: a crowned lion on hind legs, holding a cross in his paws.

The inscription, flanking the lion, reads: "Владимерской" ("of Vladimir").
On the slopes of the colours there are placed dragons with spiral tails.
The colours is rather long: 2.5 m, but it is not large when compared with the
standards. The size of standards sometimes reached 4×2 m.
Russian regiments had many standards: there were royal, regimental,
voivodian ones, the standards of different military units, standards of
"sotnia" (cossack squadron), of Strelitz regiments. Besides, there were signs
and colours belonged to military sub-units.
In the mid-17th century the standards were painted in the workshops of the
Armoury. Simon Ushakov (1628-86), Spiridon Grigoriev, and the others
were reckoned in the Armoury as well-known artists.

88. PISTOLS. 17TH CENTURY. MADE BY CRAFTSMEN OF ARMOURY
From top to bottom

PISTOL

Steel, wood, ivory. Chasing, gilding, encrustation
Total length 86 cm; weight 1.535 kg; calibre 12 mm
From the basic collection. Indexed in 1685

PISTOL

Steel, wood, mother-of-pearl. Chasing, gilding, encrustation
Total length 41.6 cm; weight 0.762 kg; calibre 12 mm
From the basic collection. Indexed in 1685

PISTOL

Steel, wood, ivory. Chasing, gilding, encrustation
Total length 54.4 cm; weight 0.925 kg; calibre 14 mm
From the basic collection

PISTOL

Steel, walnut. Chasing, gilding, encrustation, enamel
Total length 57.5 cm; weight 0.940 kg; calibre 15 mm
From the basic collection. Indexed in 1685

The pistols of Russian work of the 17th century have the excellent decoration. The barrels are cut in *repoussé* and gilded; the hilts and gun-stocks are
encrusted with mother-of-pearl and ivory. The pistols were charged just
as rifles: a portion of powder was poured into the muzzle hole, then a bullet
was driven in by the ramrod. Such pistols could reach their object at a
distance of 50 feet. The aim was taken, according at the level of the facet.
As a rule, these pistols were made twin and fastened to a saddle in the special holsters.

89. GUN-"TYUFIAK" OF TSAR ALEXEI MIKHAILOVICH. MATCHLOCK.
1654. MADE BY GRIGORI VIATKIN

Length of barrel 111 cm; calibre 18 mm; weight of gun 16 kg; weight of barrel 11.720 kg
From the basic collection. Indexed in 1685
The inscription on the barrel tells that this gun was made in the Armoury to order of the
Tsar Alexei Mikhailovich by the master Grigori Viatkin

The armourer Grigori Viatkin was indexed in the lists of the Armour
Department since 1649 till 1688
This fire-arm is called after the Turkish name "tyufiak", or "tufnek", which
means a heavy rifled large-calibre carbine used when defending fortresses or
hunting big animal.
The matchlock of the carbine has a flint-striker that was usual for the first
half of the 17th century. The cocking-piece has the shape of a monster head
with a flint for kindling fire in its teeth. The main-spring and the spring under the steel are outward, straight. At a smooth plate of the lock are the
engraved hunting scenes. A safety trigger has the shape of a sea-horse. All
details of the lock are damascened and engraved; the oak barrel is encrusted
in ivory and mother-of-pearl.

90, 91. GUNNER "ALAM". 17TH CENTURY. MADE BY CRAFTSMEN OF
MOSCOW KREMLIN

Iron. Forging, chasing, carving
Diameter 30 cm
From the basic collection

The "alam" is a breast-plate of Russian artillery-man in the 17th century.
The gunners wore the "alams" on their breasts and backs for they were the

distinctive signs of sub-unit commanders and, at the same time, the defensive equipment taking the place of the former "zertsalos" (cuirass). The
"alams" sewn on the leather or quilted wadden caftan, were trimmed with
a fringe and gilded silver lace.

92.93. "POKROVETS" OF "SAADAK" FROM GRAND ROBES OF STATE OF
TSAR MIKHAIL FEODOROVICH. FIRST QUARTER 17TH CENTURY. MADE
BY CRAFTSMEN OF ARMOURY

Canvas, satin, wire-drawn gold and silver, pearls. Embroidery
Length 175 cm; width 100 cm; weight 2.200 kg. Coat of arms (fragment): height 20 cm;
width 22 cm
From the basic collection. Indexed in 1685

The "pokrovets" covered the Tsar "saadak" (case for a bow and quiver for
arrows). In its centre there is the royal coat of arms: a double eagle with the
coat of arms of Moscow (St George and the Dragon). The border is embroidered with coat of arms of cities of former principalities and kingdoms:
of Kazan, Astrakhan, Siberia, Perm, Viatka, Bolgaria, Nizhni Novgorod,
Ryazan, Rostov, which were joined in the early 17th century to the Russian
State.
The special craftsmen, the so-called "saadachniks", or "strochniks", worked
in the Armoury. The coat of arms of Ryazan (warrior holding a naked sword)
and the embroidered inscription "The seal of Ryazan" are concluded in a
cartouche bordered with large pearls.

94, 95. "SAADAK" FROM GRAND ROBES OF STATE OF TSAR MIKHAIL
FEODOROVICH. CASE FOR BOW. QUIVER FOR ARROWS. 1628. MADE BY
CRAFTSMEN OF ARMOURY

Canvas, gold, gems, wire-drawn gold. Embroidery, chasing, enamel
Case for bow: height 75 cm; width 35 cm. Quiver: height 50 cm; width 22 cm
From the basic collection. Indexed in 1685

The "saadak" was made by the craftsmen specially invited from Germany
and by the Russian craftsman Avraam Yuriev. They worked since August
of 1627 till November of 1628. The German craftsmen were awarded by the
Tsar with "ten arshins of Damask silk and four arshins of cherry-coloured
broadcloth", i.e. about 15 roubles in all, though Avraam Yuriev received
three times less.
The "saadak" was displayed on great occasions, such as the coronations,
or when receiving ambassadors, and others. A boyard of the highest rank
usually stood by the "saadak" which was considered a great honour
The case for the bow has the coat of arms of Moscow upon it (St George slaying the Dragon) distinguishes the whole. The open-worked golden ornament,
surrounding the coat of arms, is covered with transparent glazed enamel of
soft bruish, greenish, white and red shades. The case for the bow and the
quiver are decorated with control stamps, bearing the royal coat of arms
and several symbolical animals: the unicorn symbolizing fortune and luck,
the lion with a sword, symbolizing military power, the eagle with the
crown and the gryphon with the orb, symbolizing the royal power.

96. GRAND ROBES OF STATE OF TSAR MIKHAIL FEODOROVICH. CAP
OF STATE. SCEPTRE. ORB. 1627-8. MADE IN WORKSHOPS OF MOSCOW
KREMLIN

Gold, gems, pearls, sable. Chasing, carving, enamel
Cap of State: height 30 cm; diameter 21 cm; weight 1.978 kg. Orb: height 41.5 cm;
diameter 19.4 cm; weight 2.955 kg. Sceptre: length 69,8 cm; weight 0.928 kg
From the basic collection

The Grand Robes of State consist of the Cap of State, the orb, the sceptre,
the saddle and the "saadak". The Grand Robes of State belonged to the
Tsar Mikhail Feodorovich (1596-1645) was made in the workshops of the
Moscow Kremlin by goldsmiths and other craftsmen. There are twenty na-
mes of foreign and Russian craftsmen mentioned in the records. The Boyard
V.I. Streshnev and the Dyak E. Telepnev were supervising the process.
Gold and gems were dealt out from the Tsar's Treasury.
The principal idea in all these masterpieces is performed in Russian tradi-
tions, though the German craftsmen added some accomplishments of their
own jewel treatment.
The Cap of State which was called in the documents of the 17th century "the
Cap made under supervision of Efim Telepnev", is embellished with en-
amel, gems and pearls. There are more than 150 precious stones on the Cap
of State.
The orb resembles Western traditions more than other articles of the Grand
Robes of State, particularly when treating the four scenes of biblical King
David's life, worked in *repoussé* and made in coloured enamel.

97. DIAMOND CAP OF STATE OF TSAR PETER THE GREAT. 1682-9. MADE IN WORKSHOPS OF MOSCOW KREMLIN

Silver, diamonds, gems, sable
Height (with cross) 29 cm; diameter 20 cm; weight 1.419.5 kg
From the basic collection

Russian jewellers in Moscow had reached the summit of skill in diamond work when designing the Caps of State for the coronation of two infant tsars, Peter Alexeevich (1672—1725), and his brother Ivan Alexeevich (1666-91). The complicated design of stylized flowers, crowns and double eagles over the diadem of Peter the Great is made up with diamonds. The entire diamond surface consists of 800 diamonds of various sides and shapes. The diverse faceting of diamonds results the unique play of colour and light. The lower part of the Cap of State is ornamented with cabochons of rubies, emeralds, tourmalines, on high metal stalks. The Cap of State is completed by a four-ended cross fixed on a cabochon of a tourmaline with a silver diamonded rim. The Cap of State is known as the Monomachos Cap of the Minor Robes of State belonged to Peter the Great.

98. HOLSTER. 17TH CENTURY. MADE BY CRAFTSMEN OF CAVALRY OFFICE

Leather, velvet, gold and silver thread, pearls, gems. Ornamentation in pearls
Came from the Cavalry Office between 1720-35

The holster is a case for pistols. On the flap, below the crowns, we see a double eagle in a setting which means that the holster belonged to a member of the royal family. The eagle is embroidered in pearls, with almandine eyes and an emerald on the breast. The setting is made with gold thread, the field is sprinkled with gold. The sides of the holster are bordered with the silver lace stressing its shape. The plant design embroidered with wire-drawn gold and silver covers the reverse side of the holster. The holster has the size of a pistol kept in it. A saddle of a ceremonial horse had usually two holsters.

99. DETAILS OF CEREMONIAL TSAR HORSE'S TRAPPINGS. 17TH CENTURY. MADE BY CRAFTSMEN OF CAVALRY OFFICE

BREAST-STRAP ("PAPERST")
Gold, gems. Enamel

"JINGLING CHAINS"
Silver

NECK-TASSEL "NAUZ"
Wood, pearls, silver thread

STIRRUPS
Gilded silver. Enamel, chasing

CHALDAR
Italian fabric
Ornamentation in pearls
Altabas, gold, jewels, pearls. Hand-weaving, embroidery
Length 160 cm; width 145 cm

The gold breast-strap is decorated with diamonds and blue enamel. The "jingling chains", hanging down from the pommel of a saddle, produced the gentle ring at the slightest stir of a horse. The saddle is very beautiful because of many-coloured enamel. The pad of the saddle is embroidered with pearls and uncut emeralds. The favourite Russian ornament ("gorodki") at the border made of pearls proves that the saddle was produced in Moscow.
The chaldar, made of gorgeous Italian altabas, is bordered with embroidery in pearls of Russian work. The ornament of large flowers is richly decorated with pearls, *repoussé* gold plates, rubies and emeralds.

100. "BRATINA" OF DYAK MIKHAIL DANILOV. FIRST THIRD 17TH CENTURY. MADE IN WORKSHOPS OF MOSCOW KREMLIN

Gilded silver. Chasing, carving
Diameter 12.5 cm; height 12.8 cm
From the basic collection
Granted by the Tsar Mikhail Feodorovich (1596-1645) to the Dyak Mikhail Fcofilaktovich Danilov in 1630

The "bratina" is a ball-shaped metal vessel for drinking, used at feasts. In early Russia it was used chiefly as a grace-cup and a loving cup. Full of mead, a drink, it was handed from one guest to another, keeping up peace and friendship. Hence, its name derived from the word "brother".
The "bratina" of the Dyak Mikhail Danilov is the only one known as being presented. The inscription alongside its edges says that it was presented by the Tsar for the true service of the Dyak Mikhail, son of Danila. Made in pure Russian traditions, it is distinguished by almost classical forms and clear proportions. In order to embellish the design, all intervening spaces between the vegetation are filled with shining dots, the very thing that testifies it to belong to the first half of the 17th century.

101. DIPPER OF TSAR MIKHAIL FEODOROVICH. FIRST HALF 17TH CENTURY. MADE IN WORKSHOPS OF MOSCOW KREMLIN

Silver. Chasing, carving, forging
Length (with handle) 30 cm; height (with handle) 13.2 cm; width 21 cm
From the basic collection

The gold and silver boat-shaped dippers known to be a very old form of Russian drinking vessels. These dippers were used at feasts filled with mead, a liquor widely spread in early Russia. A red mead was drunken from the gold dippers, a white mead from the silver ones.
Plain, ungilded, forged from a silver-leaf, the dipper of the Tsar Mikhail Feodorovich is remarkable because of his simple and exquisite form. Under the handle and on the outward side of the spout is a carved inscription, the only decoration of the vessel, and two trefoliate rosettes in roundels on the sides of the dipper. The outlines of it resemble a swimming swan or a boat, so the dippers of similar shape in early Russia were called swan-dippers.

102. DIPPER OF TSAR MIKHAIL FEODOROVICH. 1624. MADE BY TRETYAK PESTRIKOV AND SON. GOLD HALL

Gold, gems, pearls, niello. Casting, chasing, carving
Length (with handle) 29 cm; height (with handle) 14.2 cm; width 20.5 cm

Solid, with the broad plain bottom and the low brim, the dipper of the Tsar Mikhail Feodorovich (1596—1645) resembles the majestical swan, so exceptionally gracious, calm and gentle it looks. Casted from a gold-leaf, ornamented with gems, niello and pearls, the vessel is made in the best Russian traditions of the late 17th century. Sapphires and tourmalines in high "nest" settings are conspicuous for colour against the twinkling field of smooth gold. The nielloed inscription, written in fine Slavonic characters, ornaments the borders of the dipper and completes the whole decor of the vessel which belongs to festive utensils of the 17th century.

103. FUNERAL "BRATINA" OF TSAR MIKHAIL FEODOROVICH. FIRST HALF 17TH CENTURY. MADE IN WORKSHOPS OF MOSCOW KREMLIN

Gilded silver. Niello, chasing, carving
Height 8 cm; width 11.8 cm
From the basic collection
Along the edges of the bowl, between four carved control stamps, is placed the inscription in niello saying that this "bratina" was intended for the coffin of the Grand Prince Ivan Ivanovich, son of the Tsar Ivan the Terrible

Low, wide, of medium size, this silver "bratina" belongs to the so-called "funeral" bowls filled with water and mead, usually placed upon the coffin of the deceased. The "bratina" is made in the best traditions of the 17th century. The main beauty of the bowl is its exquisitely simple, symmetrical form and the modest brilliance of the decoration. The plain body of the "bratina" is covered with figured nielloed vegetation pattern and ornamental braided control stamps called the "kafimsky" knots.

104. TRIPTYCH WITH THE ICON "THE VIRGIN ELEUSA" OF DUMA DYAK IVAN GRIAZEV. FIRST THIRD 17TH CENTURY. MADE IN WORKSHOPS OF MOSCOW KREMLIN

Tempera on wood. Gold, silver, gems, pearls. Enamel, chasing, carving
Triptych with closed folds: height 30 cm; width 16.7 cm
Triptych with opened folds: width 33 cm. Icon: height 22 cm; width 14.8 cm
Came from the Simonov Monastery in 1918
Former property of the Duma Dyak of the Embassy Ivan Kirillovich Griazev (died 1634)

The gold mounting of the icon is decorated with the rich plant ornament in *repoussé* and coloured enamel. Though modest in colours, the enamel is in harmony with the glittering gems upon the headband and the crown, as well as with the opaque twinkling of pearl decorations hanging from the headband reaching the shoulders, like those worn by the women of the royal family in the 16th—17th century. The painting of the icon and clear shades of enamel suiting so well to the soft glamour cast by silver, gold, pearls and gems make it the perfect work of art. The icon is put into the silver triptych, the folds of which are decorated with the carved images of the Archangels at full length.

105. CROSS. 1636. THE PECHERSKY MONASTERY IN NIZHNI-NOVGOROD. REVERSE SIDE

Silver. Chasing, carving
Height 31 cm; width of upper cross-bar 15.1 cm
Came from the Blagoveschensky Monastery in Nizhni-Novgorod (presently Gorky) in 1626

Upon the reverse side of this silver chancel cross is the carved composition "The Angel Disturbing Water in a Font". The cross is an outstanding masterpiece of Russian artists and engravers. The artist who made the picture had perfectly comported the image of the Angel with the form of the cross. The engraver has achieved it by means of strong graceful lines of the contours making them voluminous and stressed the outlines with light hat ching. The picture is remarkable for the free charm that it conveys thanks to the sure hand that engraved it. This type of carving was characteristic for Russian art of the period.

106. "ENDOVA" OF BOYARD VASSILI STRESHNEV. 1644. MADE BY CRAFTSMEN OF SILVER HALL

Silver. Chasing, carving, "kanfarenye"
Diameter 28 cm; height 16.5 cm
Came from the Museum Fund in 1922
Made by the best craftsmen of the Kremlin workshops to order of the Boyard Vassili Ivanovich Streshnev who was in charge of the Armoury and Gold and Silver Halls from 1630 to 1638; between 1634 and 1645 was entrusted with various diplomatic assignments

The "endova" is a large, ball-shaped drinking vessel with a spout intended for mead, beer and kvass. Liquors were poured from the "endova" in smaller cups ("charka") and goblets ("bratina"). The body of the vessel is *repoussé* with large twisted spoon-shaped depressions, alternatively some plain and some ornamented with the finest vegetation design. This interchange of plain and ornamented curved decorations seems to give this exceedingly beautiful vessel a violent spiral motion restrained by the plain broad edges at the top; adorned with the carved incsription, it tells of the place and time of its production, as well as of ownership.
This ornamental style was on the increase in the 17th century tending to become more pompous and complicated.

107. GLASS. SECOND HALF 17TH CENTURY. MADE IN WORKSHOPS OF MOSCOW KREMLIN

Gilded silver. Chasing, carving, niello
Height 20 cm
From the basic collection

A tall plain silver gilded glass in strict simple proportions with bright gilded pattern depicts flowers spreading freely in front of a background with the slightest nielloed grasses. The realistically designed flowers on long stalks bend under the birds who perch upon them. At the base of the glass, under the flowers we see running wild animals as if in a forest, which makes the fancy ornament very picturesque; all this tells that the artistic style in Russia is approaching the style of baroque.

108. "TAREL". 1664. MADE IN WORKSHOPS OF MOSCOW KREMLIN

Gold, gems. Enamel, chasing
Diameter 21.3 cm
Came from the Patriarch Vestry in 1922
Contributed by the Boyarynia A. I. Morozova into the Chudov Monastery in 1664

The enamelled composition in the centre of the "tarel" (a church plate) shows the Sacred Cross with the city and wall of Jerusalem on the background. This style of enamel was peculiar for Russian art in Moscow in the second half of the 17th century. Beyond the castellated wall is a fancy city with beautiful palaces, cogged towers, gabled roofs and golden church domes. The city resembles early Russian architectural ensembles, such as the

Moscow Kremlin and the Kolomensky Palace. The plain edges of the plate are decorated with large sapphires and tourmalines, as well as with the nielloed inscription with the words of a prayer.

109, 110, 111, 112. BOWLS AND PLATES. LAST THIRD 17TH CENTURY. SOLVYCHEGODSK

Silver. Ussolye enamel
Diameter 16 cm
From the basic collection

The Solvychegodsk bowls, plates, boxes, etc. usually represent the images of youths and girls, birds, fantastic beings, allegorical and biblical scenes adopted from Western engravings, illustrations and "luboks". The pictures reflecting the life of the people took a customary form in this type of work. Sometimes the artists added to them fantastic pictures, ornamentations and explanatory inscriptions of their own, thus making them exceedingly interesting and conspicuous. The usual ornamentation consists of large tulips with large stalks, irises, camomiles, sunflowers; their leaves gathered them to a never-ending wreath harmonizing with the form of the vessel or box upon which they are found. Colours are gay, sunny: pale-yellow, pinkish-violet, bright-blue and greenish, with black enamelled veins.
These Ussolye enamels are distinguished for their plain snowy-white background covering the silver vessel upon which a multicoloured design is plotted in the special method of fine hatching, with special paints.
For fixing enamel on the surface the Ussolye craftsmen often resorted to filigree which at the same time embellished the bowls and plates.

113. PANAGIA OF PATRIARCH JOASAPH II
SETTING. 1671. MADE BY MIKHAIL YAKOVLEV
CAMEO. 12TH CENTURY. BYZANTIUM

Chrysoprase, gold, gems, pearls, enamel
Height 9 cm; width 9 cm
From the basic collection
Made to order of the Patriarch Joasaph II (1667-72) by Mikhail Yakovlev. the craftsman of the Patriarch Gold Hall, in 1671

The panagia is decorated with gems and multicoloured enamel, transparent and opaque both, as well as with painting in enamel. By the artistic traditions of the second half of the 17th century the principal decoration were gems, emeralds in particular which were favoured at that time for their green colour. The centre of the panagia is adorned with the Byzantine cameo of the 12th century, with the carved picture "The Dormition" made on chrysoprase.
The reverse side of the setting is bordered with the filigree plant ornament filled with white, blue, emerald-green, black, yellow and crimson enamel. Mikhail Yakovlev worked over this panagia more than one year.

114. BOWL OF TSAR ALEXEI MIKHAILOVICH. 1653. MADE IN WORKSHOPS OF MOSCOW KREMLIN

Gold, gems. Enamel, chasing, carving
Height 8.4 cm; diameter 14.9 cm
From the basic collection
Presented to the Tsar Alexei Mikhailovich (1629-76) by the Patriarch Nicon in 1653

Along the broad edges of the bowl in between large sapphires and emeralds there is the presentation inscription in black enamel. The bowl has the form of an opening flower. Its surface with large spoon-shaped depressions embossed in high relief is covered nearly everywhere with transparent emerald-green enamel, which is the background for flowers in opaque enamel. Green enamel is so deep and bright that rivals with the brilliant colour of the emeralds which placed among sapphires, rubies and diamonds completes the whole décor of the vessel.
At the bottom of the stand there is a carved inscription telling that in 1686 the tsars-brothers Peter and Ivan had presented the Prince Vassili Vassilievich Golitsyn with this bowl "for his service in making the ever-lasting peace with the Polish King". A few years later Golitsyn fell into disgrace and his property was confiscated, the bowl was returned with other valuables into the Royal Palace.

115 ICON "THE TRINITY" IN MOUNTING. 1676-82. MADE IN WORKSHOPS OF MOSCOW KREMLIN

Gold, diamonds. Enamel, chasing
Height 28.2 cm; width 22.8 cm
Came from the Royal Palace in 1922

In the second half of the 17th century Russian art tended to gay, bright colours, to superfluous pomp which revealed buoyancy of the patterns; such is the style of this icon.

"The Trinity" upon the icon is made after the biblical legend about the three angels visiting Abraham and his wife Sarah.

The mounting covers nearly all the figures leaving only faces, feet and hands of the saints. The background of the mounting is run with transparent bright-green enamel; the *repoussé* clothes of the saints are covered with enamel both transparent and opaque, of bright rich tints. The glittering diamonds on the nimbi of the saints add to the splendour of this fancy colour range. The plain golden framing, ornamented only with the superposed flower rosettes in enamel, counterbalances and deadens the luxurious central part of the mounting.

116. SAKKOS OF PATRIARCH PITIRIM. SECOND HALF 17TH CENTURY. MADE IN TSARINA'S WORKSHOP

Italian fabric
Ornamentation in pearls of Russian work
Silk brocaded, velvet, pearls, coloured silks, gold thread. Handweaving
Length 127.0 cm; width (with sleeves) 155.0 cm
Came from the Patriarch Vestry in 1920

The sakkos is one of the rare masterpieces of Italian hand-weaving as well as a specimen of the extraordinary skill of Russian milliners. The design on brocaded silk is typical for Italian fabric of the 18th century. Harmony of a white field with bright silks and the shining gold produces the impression of freshness and festival brightness of spring. The sakkos looks as if it is enframed in a gorgeous setting of crimson velvet; upon it with "Kaffa" pearls are embroidered the words of a prayer. Mostly decorative is the embroidery on the sleeves. Figures of saints, entirely interwoven with gold thread, seem to be worked in *repoussé*, and the colour of the numerous designs are so bright that they produce the impression of being made in enamel.

117. GOSPELS. COVER. 1678. MADE BY CRAFTSMEN OF GOLD HALL MIKHAIL VASSILIEV, IONA SIMIDEL, YURI AND STEPAN NYRINS, GOLIASH, CHRISTIAN KREIMER, DIAMOND-MASTER DMITRI TERENTIEV AND MASTER-ENAMELLER YURI FROBOS

Gold, silver, gems. Chasing, enamel, niello, carving, "kanfarenye"
Height 47 cm; width 33.5 cm

The décor of the cover of the Gospels is a perfect specimen of Russian designs which were exceedingly common in the second half of the 17th century. The face of the gold cover is decorated with the *repoussé* images of the saints made in multicoloured enamel. Articles of clothings, the architecture of the buildings, furniture and the "implements of Passion" placed in oval gold plaques upon the middle part of the cover are all run with transparent enamel, while the faces of the saints, details of their clothes, fragments of the background and architecture buildings are covered with opaque coloured enamel. The background of the middle portion of the cover is ornamented with large tulips embossed in low relief, the usual design of the period. This decoration is rendered richer by the gems in gold chased casts, the nimbi of the saints besprinkled with diamonds and by the narrow jewelled rims winding around the centre and the corners of the cover.

118, 119, 120, 121. GOSPELS. 1678. MINIATURES MADE BY ARTISTS OF ARMOURY: FEODOR ZUBOV, IVAN MAXIMOV, SERGEI VASSILIEV, PAVEL NIKITIN, FEODOR YURIEV, MAKAR POTAPOV AND MAXIM IVANOV

Water-colour and gold on paper. Pen, brush
Size of leaf: height 44.5 cm; width 32.2 cm

This Gospels book with 1,200 illustrations in water-colour and gold and a great quantity of head-pieces, colophons and initials was produced, according to the chronicles, during eight months of night and day work. Though the illustrations are painted by different masters but they are all made in one artistic style. They are distinguished for their beauty of ornaments, for its vividness tending towards real life, even when they lead to fanciful drawings.

When illustrating a parable that is worded on the same page the artists show it as a common scene taken from life. The landscapes become whole pictures with woods, meadows and rivers. The contours of gorgeous fantastic buildings become the principal object of this composition. The earth-borns are painted next to the saints. The miniatures of the 1678 Gospels are drawn with pen and painted in water-colours and gold. The colouring is joyous and light. The legend "The Nativity" is illustrated with two scenes: below is the grotto where, according to the legend, Christ was born; above, the biblical city of Bethlehem. On the upper miniature next to the towers of Gothic

mould stands an early Russian chapel, and a church with an onion dome comports with the buildings of the Renaissance. The Magi at the walls of the city resemble rather rich merchants than saint sages.

The philosophical parable about the sower at the top of the leaf is performed in a scene of peaceful peasant life; the sower is below (at the bottom of the page). In the legend about St John the Baptist (the scene of Herod talking to the chief priests and scribes), the artist takes the spectator into the perspective viewed through an arch where the city is painted. In the miniatures of Herod's feast and the decapitation of St John the Baptist the artist paints crowds of people in different planes.

122. ICON "THE VIRGIN OF VLADIMIR" WITH TWELVE CHURCH FEASTS. MID-17TH CENTURY. MADE IN TSARINA'S WORKSHOP

Russian icon embroidery
Linen, gold and silver thread, coloured silks
Comes from the Patriarch Vestry in 1920
Length 109 cm; width 74.0 cm

The icon is made in Tsarina's Workshop. It is embroidered with twisted silk, the background, the robes and haloes resemble those icons which were nearly all covered with gold mountings and only the faces and hands were exposed. The Virgin and Child on the present icon are embroidered with twisted silks of light brown shades. The different technique of embroidery turned into beautiful geometrical designs reminding the engravings and *repoussé* patterns on gold- and silverware of the 17th century.

Pictures of twelve Church Feasts make a splendid frame around the icon. They are: Annunciation, Nativity, Presentation in the Temple, Baptism, Entry into Jerusalem, Crucifixion, Dormition, Descent of the Holy Spirit, Ascension, Resurrection, Transfiguration, and Raising of Lazarus.

123. PALL FOR SEPULCHRE OF METROPOLITAN JONAH OF MOSCOW. 1657

Russian icon embroidery
Damask, wire-drawn gold and silver, gold and silver thread, coloured silks
Length 2.50 m; width 97 cm
Came from the Dormition Cathedral in the Moscow Kremlin in 1920
Contributed by G.D. Stroganov into the Dormition Cathedral in the Moscow Kremlin

This pall belongs to the so-called Stroganov School of embroidery and dates from the period of its flourishing in the field of art.

The traditional composition on the pall pictures the Metropolitan Jonah canonized in the 16th century standing upright, full face. The figure in lengthy proportions is very impressive, the face does not lack individual features performed by the skilful hand of a gifted artist. The face of Jonah is embroidered in pale silks; the darker threads of silk stress the contours but do not interfere with the general meaning of the picture. The embroidery in gold and silver threads repeats the "crescent" patterns of the late-Byzantine fabrics. The border of the pall is embroidered with a liturgical canticle. The inscription on the red Damask lining tells about its production to order of Grigori Dmitrievich Stroganov.

It took nearly four years for the milliner to embroider such a pall.

124. STOLE. 17TH CENTURY. DETAIL. MADE IN TSARINA'S WORKSHOP

Russian icon embroidery
Velvet, pearls, gems
Length 107 cm; width 36 cm
Came from the Novospassky Monastery in 1924
Contributed by the Tsar Mikhail Feodorovich (1596-1645) into the Novospassky Monastery

The type of embroidery of this stole is a general characteristic of all Russian decorative applied art in the mid- and second half of the 17th century. The rich plant design thickly ornamented with gold, pearls and gems is exceptionally beautiful. The technique of embroidery was perfect. The floral pattern of the tissue is nearly all covered with pearls, adorned with shining diamonds and embroidered with gold spangles. In the centre of the stole are gold faceted buttons ornamented with bright enamel and rubies.

125. PHELONION. 17TH CENTURY. DETAIL

Ornamentation in pearls of Russian work
Italian fabric
Plain hexamite, velvet, pearls, gems, gold. Hand-weaving
Yoke: length 90 cm; height 32 cm
Came from the Museum Fund, Moscow Region, in 1930
Contributed by the Tsar Mikhail Feodorovich into the Novospassky Monastery

The phelonion of Italian plain hexamite was made in Tsarina's Workshop at the period when the producing capacity of this workshop was the greatest. It was decorated with embroidery which thanks to its beauty and technique may be regarded as the gem of creative power in the art of Russian artists and milliners. Seventeenth century embroidery designs were predominantly floral and there were endless variations. Russian embroiderers achieved magnificence and a high degree of beauty by the careful grading of pearls and the clever use of gems.

The curved pearl stalks of tulips with rich leaves and manypetalled flowers are freely spread around the central cross made of large emeralds and diamonds of medium size. The various size of pearls raises the design and adds to it the beautiful play of light and shade. Brilliancy of the diamonds in the hearts of the tulips is maintained by the festive colouring of the central composition. The gold spangles filling the blank spaces make an interesting combination between the luxurious pearl design and the black velvet background.

126. INFANT HOODED COACH OF PETER THE GREAT. SECOND HALF 17TH CENTURY. MADE BY CRAFTSMEN OF CAVALRY OFFICE

Spanish leather
Oak, leather, mica, lead, taffeta, iron. Stamping, gilding
Height 120 cm; length 150 cm; width 75 cm
Came from the Coach Court before 1834

INFANT HOODED SLEDGE OF PETER THE GREAT. SECOND HALF 17TH CENTURY. MADE BY CRAFTSMEN OF CAVALRY OFFICE

Spanish leather
Oak, leather, mica, lead, taffeta, iron. Stamping, gilding
Came from the Coach Court before 1834

I.E. Zabelin writes about the hooded sledge of Peter the Great (1671—1725): "In the month of May, 1675 the Boyard Artamon Sergeevich Matveev asked the Tsarevich Peter to do him honour and accept a little coach and four horses together with velvet breech-bands, gilded buckles and embroidered horse-clothes for their bangs, manes and tails".

The Secretary of Viennese Embassy Lieseck saw how Peter the Great at the age of three was taken to the Trinity-Sergius Monastery: "A small carriage, all decorated with gold, was drawn by four horses of pygmean breed, accompanied by four dwarfs at the sides and one at the rear on horseback upon a tiny horse".

The infant hooded vehicles of Peter the Great were usually called the "amusing" ones ("poteshny").

According to the fashion of the period, such coaches were upholstered with leather, stamped in gold with vegetation patterns on the light-blue and red background; inward they were covered with red taffeta. Little windows were made of mica, the lead of its frames laid in different directions made a various design for every window.

The summer coach has nearly modern rotating front sections, the winter one was put on runners.

127. "PLATNO" OF PETER THE GREAT. 17TH CENTURY

Italian brocade
Plain hexamite, silver lace
Length 165.5 cm; width of hem 380 cm; length of sleeve 52 cm
From the basic collection
Once a property of Peter the Great (1671-1725)

The "platno" is the richest ceremonial robe of Russian tsars intended for coronations, state receptions, royal entertainments, etc.

These robes were not mentioned in the documents before 1628, though Russian grand princes and tsars were portrayed in similar dresses already in the 16th century.

The ceremonial robes of tsars were made at those times of imported precious fabrics: brocade, velvet, hexamite trimmed with rare furs, gold buttons, clasps and lace. The "platno" is a rectangular long shirt with broad sleeves reaching the elbows.

The "platno" of Peter the Great is of another cut: it is narrower above and very broad below. According to the Inventories of the Tsar's Treasury, it is known that but for silver bone-lace kept intact to the present time, Peter's robe has the sable trimming, six emerald buttons and other decorations. The interwoven inscription on the sleeve tells that the "platno" was made of Venetian plain brocade.

This luxurious tissue was presented to Peter the Great by the Hetman of Ukraina Mazepa (1644—1709) when visiting Moscow in 1689.

128, 129. MONOMACHOS CAP OF STATE. LATE 13TH—EARLY 14TH CENTURY. ORIENT

Gold, gems, pearls, sable. Filigree
Height (with cross) 18.4 cm; diameter 19.8 cm
From the basic collection

The Monomachos Cap of State is the crown transmitted by inheritance from one Russian tsar to his descendants. There are several versions regarding its origin. Some historians (e.g. N. Kondakov) think that it is of Byzantine work, others (e.g. A. Spitsyn) think it of middle-Asiatic origin, the third version (e.g. G. Filimonov) proves it to be of Arabian work.

The records mentioned this Cap of State in the Treasury of Ivan Kalita under the name of the "gold" one. But the name of "Monomachos" was given to it in 1498 after the coronation of Dmitri, the grandson of the Grand Prince Ivan III (1440—1505). A legend is that in the late 15th century it was sent together with other Byzantine regalia by Emperor Constantine Monomachos to the Kievan Prince Vladimir Monomachos. Actually, this legend bears the political idea of the time, that autocratic power was transmitted to the Moscow Princes from the Kievan Princes who had received it from Byzantine emperors. This legend is represented in detail in the carved compositions which ornamented the throne of Ivan IV the Terrible in the Dormition Cathedral of the Moscow Kremlin. The latest coronation in which this Cap of State was used took place in 1682 when the brother of Peter the Great, Ivan Alexeevich was coronated.

130. DAMASK STEEL SHIELD OF BOYARD FEODOR MSTISLAVSKY. 16TH CENTURY. MADE BY MUMIN-MOHAMMED. IRANIAN AZERBAIJAN

Damask steel, turquoise, gold. Forging, polishing, encrustation
Diameter 508 cm; weight 2,200 kg
From the basic collection. Indexed in 1685
Came into Tsar's Treasury in April 1622, after the death of the Prince Feodor Ivanovich Mstislavsky, well-known voivode under Ivan the Terrible (1530-84)

The connoisseurs in Oriental arms and armament consider this shield to be superior to all other specimen of this kind known in the world for its fine workmanship and artistic taste.

The shield is hammered from "red" Damask steel. The surface is *repoussé* in forty-two oblique concave polished bands; every other is encrusted with gold. Some bands are ornamented with gold, the others are patterned with the finest designs (battle-pieces and hunting scenes, men, birds and animals). Several scenes are taken from the epics "Leilah and Mejnun" by Nizami (c. 1141-c. 1203), the greatest Azerbaijanian poet: Mejnun with a hare in the desert, a bare guiding a camel on the lead, etc. One of the oblique bands bears in the cartouche the hall-mark with a name of a master: "Made by Mumin-Mohammed Zerneshan". The last word means in Azerbaijanian language "a metal master".

131. CEREMONIAL BROADSWORDS. 17TH CENTURY
From left to right

BROADSWORD. ORIENT

Damask steel, wood, gilded silver, turquoise, rubies
Length (in sheath) 112 cm; weight 1,950 kg. Length of blade 92 cm; width 5 cm
From the basic collection. Indexed in 1685

BROADSWORD. RUSSIA

Damask steel, wood, velvet, gilded silver, turquoise, rubies
Length (in sheath) 108 cm; weight 1,800 kg
From the basic collection. Indexed in 1685

BROADSWORD. IRAN

Damask steel, wood, gilded silver, turquoise
Length (in sheath) 106 cm; weight 1,800 kg. Length of blade 92 cm; width 4.7 cm

BROADSWORD. ORIENT

Damask steel, wood, gilded silver, turquoise
Length (in sheath) 112 cm; weight 1,955 kg. Length of blade 92 cm; width 4,5 cm
From the basic collection. Indexed in 1685

Appeared in the 15th century in Venice, the broadswords were and later brought to the East as a battle weapon. In the 17th century the broadswords were used as a weapon for state and public occasions only. Their silver hilts were gilded and richly ornamented with gems. The wooden sheath were trimmed with velvet and decorated to match the hilts. These luxury broadswords were in harmony with the bright costly gowns of Russian boyards. In Russia, as well as in the East, the broadswords were suspended on the swords-belts horizontally, while in West-European countries (e.g. in Poland) they were suspended vertically.

132.   THRONE OF TSAR BORIS GODUNOV. LATE 16TH CENTURY. IRAN

Wood, gold, gems. "Basma"
Height 90 cm; width 51.5 cm; depth 62.5 cm
From the basic collection
Brought into Russia together with other valuable presents to the Tsar Boris Godunov (c. 1551-1605) from Iranian Shah Abbas I (1587-1628) in 1604. The court records tell that ... "the Shah (Abbas) sent the Ambassador Lachin-beg to the great ruler of Russia with the gold royal throne ornamented with rubies, emeralds and other gems formerly belonging to Persian kings".

The throne of Boris Godunov is a typical specimen of Iranian armchairs of the 16th century. Gold leaves covering the wooden frame of the throne are multicoloured with a stamped floral design and entirely disseminated with gems. The precious stones show the lines of its construction adding to it oriental splendour and colour. The bottom of the throne, inward sides of the back and elbow-rests are covered with brocade of the 18th century, the original 16th century-velvet of the throne under it.
A rosewood staff ornamented with gems is made by Iranian craftsmen of the 17th century.

133.   "DIAMOND" THRONE OF TSAR ALEXEI MIKHAILOVICH. 1659. IRAN

Silver, gold, gems
Height 161 cm; width 75.5 cm; depth 51 cm
From the basic collection
Brought to the Tsar Alexei Mikhailovich by a merchant Saradot in 1659 as a present from the Armenian Trade Company of Iran in Isfahan

The throne resembles an old-Russian armchair with a high back and elbow-rests and in one of the richest Eastern gifts in the 17th century. The gold and silver plates which cover its frame are patterned with a fine open-work ornament of stylized trefoils and elephants in *repoussé* placed in the middle of the bottom. The lower parts of the lateral sides are adorned with excellent miniatures, and the right side of the back is ornamented with embroidery on black velvet representing the two genii supporting a crown above the cartouche; a presentation inscription in Latin reads that this present should bring the Moscow Emperor Alexei Mikhailovich happiness and glory. Since the number of diamonds was more than 800, the throne has been called the "diamond".
In the minutes of 1762 regarding the arrival of the Iranian Embassy it was said that this throne valued 22,591 roubles 60 altyns. As a reward for this throne and other presents the Embassy received 4,000 in silver and 19,500 in copper.
The throne was used in the 19th century at coronations of empresses.

134.   "POKROVETS". 16TH CENTURY. DETAIL. IRAN

Panne. Hand-weaving
Width of border 28 cm
Came from the Cavalry Office between 1720-36

The fabric of this horse-cloth is woven with a scene from Nizami's poem "Leilah and Mejnun". The rapport represents Mejnun in the enchanted desert. Rare bushes are rising straight in the broiling sun; they form light spots on a light-pink background. Pheasants stalk proudly to a youth who looks pensively to afar. The finest colour gradations make the composition physically real. This horse-cloth is one of the best masterpieces of this kind of hand-weaving.
Originally this velvet used to be a "namiot" (a large horse-cloth). But in the first half of the 17th century the velvet was cut to pieces and one part of it was used as a "pokrovets" (kept now in the Armoury); the other part was used to make up a border of the published "pokrovets". Such rich horse-clothes were laid on the saddles of ceremonial horses.

135.   CAFTAN. LAST QUARTER 16TH CENTURY. IRAN

Satin, silver. Embroidery
Length 142 cm; width (of hem) 197.5 cm; length of sleeve 110.2 cm
From the basic collection

Supposed to be a property of the Tsarevich Ivan Ivanovich (1554-81), or of the Tsar Feodor Ivanovich (1557-98)

The cut of this caftan resembles the Oriental robe with long sleeves, triangular collar, without buttons or clasps. Deep-blue satin is decorated with an interwoven composition of bright silks: a youth in an Oriental short caftan and a turban, with a dagger at the belt. He is holding an enormous stone above his head. A fantastic bird is sitting on the tree, a dragon is under it. The story goes that this scene is connected with the exploits of Alexander the Great. The caftan is made of rare and precious fabric. The inventories of royal property under Ivan the Terrible, as well as those of the early 17th century mentioned such fabrics as being brought to Russia only as valuable presents.

136.   IRANIAN SADDLES AND HORSE-CLOTHES. 16TH—17TH CENTURY

Below

SADDLE OF TSAR FEODOR IVANOVICH. LATE 16TH CENTURY. IRAN

Wood, brocaded velvet, gold, gems. "Basma", hand-weaving
Came from the Cavalry Office between 1720-36
Presented to the Tsar Feodor Ivanovich (1557-98) by the Iranian Shah Abbas I (1557-1628)

SHABRACK OF TSAR MIKHAIL FEODOROVICH. FIRST HALF 17TH CENTURY. IRAN

Broadcloth, gold and silver thread. Hand-weaving, embroidery
Length 65 cm; width 146 cm
Came from the Cavalry Office between 1720-36
Presented to the Tsar Mikhail Feodorovich (1596-1645) by the Iranian Shah Abbas I

Above

SADDLE OF TSAR MIKHAIL FEODOROVICH. EARLY 17TH CENTURY. IRAN

Wood, panne, gold, gems. "Basma", hand-weaving
Came from the Cavalry Office between 1720-36
Presented to the Tsar Mikhail Feodorovich by the Iranian Shah Safi in 1635

„POKROVETS". FIRST HALF 17TH CENTURY. KASHAN, IRAN

Fabric for border produced in Turkey
Panne, satin. Hand-weaving
Came from the Cavalry Office between 1720-36

The form of a saddle for the horse of the Tsar Feodor Ivanovich is typical for Iran in the 16th century: the back arch is low and sloping, the pommel is narrow and high with a round head. The setting in gold "basma" with large turquoises and rubies is similar to the decorations on the throne of Boris Godunov kept in the Armoury. The throne and the saddle are supposed to be made in the same workshop. The saddle was in use till the late 17th century.
The saddle for the horse of the Tsar Mikhail Feodorovich set in gold "basma" is decorated with rubies, emeralds and dark-blue turquoise. The seat and splash-boards are upholstered with excellent Iranian panne. Records of the 17th century tell about this saddle the following: "It was sent together with the gifts of Kizilbash Shah in 143". In the 17th century the saddle was worth 600 roubles, an enormous sum for those times.
The horse-cloth is made of rare, very beautiful Kashanian velvet. The scale of colours (white, black, emerald-green, yellow) is typical for Iranian fabrics and fine colour gradations make the velvet picturesque, exquisite and noble. Kashanian velvet is rare in all world collections.

137.   SADDLE OF TSAR ALEXEI MIKHAILOVICH. SECOND HALF 17TH CENTURY. TURKEY

Velvet, gold, gems. Embroidery, chasing, hand-weaving
Came from the Cavalry Office between 1720-36
Presented by Constantinople merchants

"CHALDAR". 17TH CENTURY. TURKEY

Velvet. Hand-wearing
Length 138 cm; width 70 cm

The shape of a saddle for the horse of the Tsar Alexei Mikhailovich (1629-76) is typical for Turkey of the 17th century: a high pointed pommel resembling the moresque arch, a wide rear arch and a light curvature of the seating. The saddle is trimmed with crimson velvet decorated with gold jewelled plates in the shape of carnations and pomegranates bordered with pearls. The silver lace on the edges stresses the contours of the saddle.

Upon the "chaldar" (horse trappings) little "hoofs" are woven into the web in black and white; the pattern is checked.

In the years of 1630s the "hoofed" velvet was produced in Russia in the Velvet Court disposed near the Moskva River, at the outer wall of the Kremlin, between the Tainitskaya and Vodovzvodnaya Towers.

The "chaldar" consists of nine pieces of different size and form. It is known to have been the royal caftan which when worn out was altered into this "chaldar"; the caftan is supposed to belong to the Tsar Boris Godunov (c. 1551-1605).

138. "SAADAK" OF TSAR ALEXEI MIKHAILOVICH. BOW CASE. MID-17TH CENTURY. DETAIL. CONSTANTINOPLE, TURKEY

Gold, gems. Enamel
Size of bow case: height 75 cm; width 35 cm
Presented to the Tsar Alexei Mikhailovich (1629-76) by Greek merchants from Constantinople, Ivan Yuriev and Dmitri Astafiev in 1656

According to the customs of those times, a tsar owed presents of gratitude which were to be of the same value as those brought by the ambassadors. The experts invited to examine the "saadak" (bow case and quiver for arrows) valued it 6,000 roubles. But in reality the article was more expensive: it is embellished with more than 1,500 diamonds, rubies and emeralds. In the centre of the bow case is a crowned eagle ornamented with black enamel, gems and diamonds. The inscription in Greek surrounding the eagle dedicates the bow case to the Tsar, comparing him to Greek Emperor Constantine.

The quiver is decorated with the eagle of smaller size. The continuation of the inscription winds around the eagle.

139. SAKKOS. 17TH CENTURY. TURKEY

Brocaded velvet. Hand-weaving
Length 133 cm; width (with sleeves) 131 cm
Came from the Patriarch Vestry in 1920

There is a big collection of Turkish fabrics in the Armoury, with plenty of the 17th century fabrics in particular. They are patterned with large, twelve-pointed stars of dark-crimson velvet, encircled in gold thread; hence, the name of the velvet.

The same pattern is seen not only on fabrics but on glazed earthenware and tiles also.

This pattern which is rather heavy in its solidity has a contrasting scale of bright colours which are very effective, and was in the mode of Russian feudal aristocracy

Such fabrics were used in Russia for robes of tsars, boyards and high priests, for ceremonial sledge rugs, horse-clothes, for upholstering of walls and furniture, etc.

WEST-EUROPEAN ART OF
15TH-19TH CENTURIES

140, 141. TOURNAMENT ARMOUR. 15TH CENTURY. GERMANY

Iron, leather straps. Chasing, polishing
Height (with helmet) 180 cm; weight 30 kg
Came from the Hermitage in 1930

This tournament armour consists of the helmet (with the visor closing the face of a warrior), the breast-plate, the sleeves with the gauntlets, the belt and the boots. All the details, hammered from iron and gathered together with leather straps are well fitted to the size of a bearer. Thanks to a certain elasticity, the knight could stir and move in it. Ten of this type of 17th century armour are kept in the Armoury. Some of them belonged to tsars and boyards. One of them was presented to the Tsar Feodor Ivanovich (1557-98) by Polish King Stephen Batory in 1584. Two of them belonged to the Prince Ivan Alexeevich Vorotynsky and to the Boyard Nikita Ivanovich Romanov. All these armours were not intended for use in warfare. Sometimes they were worn on the official court ceremonies in the 17th century. The tournaments, so popular in Western countries in the mid-17th century, were unknown in Russia.

142. CHALICE. LATE 15TH CENTURY. GERMANY

Gilded silver. Chasing, casting, engraving, gilding
Height 24 cm; diameter of bowl 10 cm
From the basic collection

Sacred vases and luxurious church-plates were much in demand in medieval Germany; toward the end of the 15th century this demand was largely supplied by silverware. Silver was more desirable than copper, used in jewelry before, because of its beautiful natural white colour and because it was plastic and easily modelled, and also because silver yielded to gilding and polishing.

Precious silver church utensils made in Germany had often fallen under the influence of architecture which was the leading art of that time. The shape of the chalice seems to confirm this suggestion: it reveals many Gothic elements in miniature, not only of the church accessories but of the building itself. Gothic architectural designs, though continuously modifying, repeat themselves in trellises, in lancet-arches and spires, on tight-plates-nervures, in rich and complicated ornamentation on the blades of the basis, in cast openwork on the lower part of the bowl. Typical for the late Gothic style is the ornamental splendour, peculiar for the ornamentation of the chalice of the whole

143. "DÜRER" TYPE GOBLET. LATE 15TH—EARLY 16TH CENTURY. NUREMBERG, GERMANY

Gilded silver. Chasing, casting, engraving, gilding
Diameter of bowl 15.5 cm; height 35.5 cm
From the basic collection

The German "pine-apple" goblet has been copied many hundred times and can be found in numerous world collections. This favourite form of the vessel, resulted from the very technique when chasing, has become popular due to the fact that this form allowed to evoke the natural qualities of the metal. Its appearance bridged the 15th and 16th centuries and survived during more than two ages.

This goblet is the early type of what is no longer the Gothic style and could not be called the style of Renaissance. The goblet is remarkable for resembling those vessels that are usually found on sketches, drawings and pictures by Albrecht Dürer (1471—1528). It is lightly built, and the design with the rows of bumps comports with the vertical lines of the whole, as well as with the prolonged lines of its endings; the effect of its supple elements emerges in the spiral lines of the stem and its brace in the middle. The form of the vessel is broader and more flexible in comparison to the Gothic style; its horizontal band and rich designs with graceful leaves which replace the usual rigid pattern of boughs and twigs, all this proves altogether to be the forerunner on the new way of creative work of German silversmiths which resulted in brilliant new achievements.

144. BASIN. MADE BY TOBIAS KRAMER (active between 1615-34). AUGSBURG, GERMANY

Gilded silver. Chasing, casting, gilding, puncheon
Diameter 57.5 cm; height 6.2 cm
From the basic collection

The very type of a wash-basin, used not only by aristocracy but by rich town-dwellers also, is characteristic for the latest Renaissance in Germany. The basin has a specially elevated building in the centre to keep steady balance of the ewer which was brought together with it. Ornamentations in *repoussé* are placed around the building in concentric girdles. The widest of them at the bottom of the vessel is covered with mythological sea-images. When filled with water, the sea deities seemed to be in their elements. This light allegory showed that the ornamentations had to serve the use of the basin; additional ornaments always pictured the contrary theme: the earth is opposed to water, for it was a time when allegory symbols were favourable, so the gifts of the earth as bunches of fruit are chased round the brim of the basin.

145. INTERIOR OF COACH HALL
COACH OF EMPRESS ELIZAVETA PETROVNA ("COUPÉ"). 1746. MADE BY JOHANN HOPENHAUPT (1709-57). BERLIN, GERMANY

Beech, iron. Gilding on gesso ground, oil-painting, wood-carving
Height 200 cm; length 550 cm; width 250 cm
Came from the Moscow Museum of Horsebreeding in March 1926
Presented to the Empress Elizaveta Petrovna (1709-61) by the Emperor of Germany Frederic II (1744-97)

COACH OF EMPRESS CATHERINE II ("BERLINE" TYPE). 1761. MADE BY JOHN BUCKENDALE. ENGLAND

Maple, iron. Gilding on gesso ground, oil-painting, carving
Height 240 cm; length 560 cm; width 250 cm
Came from the Moscow Museum of Horsebreeding in March 1926

COACH OF EMPRESS CATHERINE II ("BERLINE" TYPE). 1765. FRANÇOIS BOUCHER SCHOOL. FRANCE

Ash-tree. Gilding on gesso ground, oil-painting, carving
Height 245 cm; length 460 cm; width 225 cm
Came from the Moscow Museum of Horsebreeding in March 1926

The body of the coach of the Empress Elizaveta Petrovna is suspended on straps, has metal cranked springs, a linking shaft, rotating front sections, a "swan-neck" and a coach-box.
Its shape of the sedan-chair is narrow at the bottom and broader towards the top which was usual for the carriages of the "*coupé*" type. The coach is richly decorated with red velvet embroidered with gold. The coach was used for the coronation visits in 1856 and 1881.
The coach of the Empress Catherine II made by Buckendale has a usual construction for the coaches of "*Berline*" type that is to say it has vertical and horizontal metal springs. The framework of the coach has two springs on both sides of the body fastened to a single platform that serves for front and back stancheons. The body of the coach has S-shaped form; the back and front walls are rectilineal.
The coach of the Empress Catherine II of 1765 was used by members of emperor family for visiting other countries during the coronations, in the years of 1826, 1856, 1881. The coach had been renovated in 1881, the front and the back walls, the shaft and the wheels were entirely gilded.

146. WEST-EUROPEAN SADDLES AND HORSE-CLOTHES IN 16TH-17TH CENTURY.

Below
SADDLE OF BORIS GODUNOV. 16TH CENTURY. POLAND
Wood, velvet, wire-drawn silver. Gilding, engraving, hand-weaving, application
Came from the Cavalry Office between 1720-36
Presented to the Tsar Boris Godunov (c. 1551-1605) by the Polish King Sigismund III (1587-1632) in 1600

"POKROVETS". 17TH CENTURY. HAMBURG, GERMANY
Velvet, gold and silver thread. Hand-weaving, embroidery
Length 62 cm; width 128 cm
Came from the Cavalry Office between 1720-36

Above
SADDLE. MADE BY ANDREAS MACKENZON. SECOND HALF 17TH CENTURY. GERMANY
Wood, velvet, gold and silver thread. Hand-weaving, embroidery, chasing

SHABRACK. 17TH CENTURY. HAMBURG, GERMANY
Velvet, gold and silver thread. Hand-weaving, embroidery
Length 81 cm; width 128 cm
Came from the Cavalry Office between 1720-36

The saddle for the horse of Boris Godunov was used in warfare. The saddle fitted closely to the horse's back was intended for the steady seat of a rider in the cuirass. The saddle is trimmed with crimson velvet and decorated with applicated Oriental signs in the shape of large sharp-pointed ovals, for Oriental art appealed to the people of Poland at that time, and with silver gilded plates. The saddle was brought to Moscow in 1600 by the Polish ambassador Leo Sapieha who visited Russia on behalf of conclusion a union between Poland and Russia. According to its rich embroidery, the saddle made by Mackenzon was intended for royal tournaments; its form is that for knightly jousts. The pommels are high, in the shape of a chair, with special cylinders what clutched a rider's feet
The shabrack is made of red velvet with the rich vegetation ornament. The embroidery "in high relief" is very expressive. Such type of embroidery was specially loved in the Germany in the 17th century.

147, 148. HELMET. MADE BY LUCIO PICCININO (ACTIVE IN 1550-1600). MILAN, ITALY

Iron. Forging, chasing, gilding
Height 41.5 cm; diameter 26 cm
From the basic collection. Indexed since 1685
Supposed to be the "gilded helmet presented to the Tsar Feodor Ivanovich (1557-98) by the Polish King Sigismund III and brought by the ambassador Paul Sapieha"

The helmet is forged from two iron plates riveted together. The helmet's crown turns into the brim without the usual crest. The broad brim unbend near vertically is turned up a little resembling the German musketeer caps of the 16th century. The front and back edges of the brim are pulled out forming peaks with tubes for fixing ostrich feathers. The sides of the helmet are worked in *repoussé* with two round medallions depicting the heroic deeds of Hercules. On one medallion there is Hercules tearing Antheus off the earth; on the other we see the battle between Hercules and a manyheaded Hydra. Above these medallions are placed a double eagle and St George slaying the Dragon (the coat of arms of Moscow).
The surface of the helmet is richly gilded, that's why it was called the "gilded helmet" in the ancient chronicles. Now, the gilding has all come off due to a fire which took place in the Royal Palace in the 18th century. The helmet was specially made by the Milanese craftsman Lucio Piccinino to be presented to the Russian Tsar.

149. CHALICE. 1330. MADE BY ANDREA ARDITI. FLORENCE, ITALY

Gilded silver. Chasing, gilding, carving, enamel
Diameter 9.2 cm; height 24 cm
From the basic collection

The unique specimen of early Italian silverware which is kept in the Armoury is one of the rarest in world collections. Though signed works of art may be found in Italy more often than in other countries of medieval Europe, each of them is an extraordinary phenomenon. The Latin inscription in black enamel on the vessel's stem reads: "Andreas Arditi da Florentia ma fecit" ("I was made by Andrea Arditi of Florence"), distinguishing it from all the others. We know very little about the craftsman. He was known to be well-qualified in his craft and was given heavy tasks, among them there were famous bust-reliquary and a mitre (for the cathedral in Florence), a cross for the merchant guild (in San-Finniato, Florence), and three chalices made in 1331 and 1338. The silversmith Arditi decorated his masterpieces with chasing and enamel. The new method of working in transparent coloured enamelling that came in from France, fitted very well in Florence where polychrome decorations had been readily used before. The chalice is embellished with transparent coloured enamels with images of saints, animals, fancy birds, ornaments and inscriptions. An opaque glittering *terra cotta* enamel covers fine indents between the flower petals on the bowl, making a sort of medallions on the apple of the stem.

150. SAKKOS OF PATRIARCH ADRIAN. 1696

Ornamentation in pearls of Russian work
Italian fabric
Brocaded velvet, pearls, gems. Hand-weaving
Length 135 cm; width (with sleeves) 134 cm
Came from the Patriarch Vestry in 1920

Hexamites and fabrics of the type were considered the most rich and beautiful in the Russia of the 17th century. They were at the disposal of the aristocracy only, so the clothes made of these fabrics were preserved with care and were usually past from one generation to another, being altered only to suit the size of the new possessor. The present fabric has the same destiny: firstly, in 1679, it was used for the ceremonial robe of the Tsar Feodor Alexeevich (1661-82). After his death it was altered for a caftan of the Tsar Ivan Alexeevich (1666-96), and in 1696 it was used for the sakkos of the Patriarch Adrian. The text of the origin of this sakkos is embroidered in pearls around the collar. The ornamentation in pearls and gems made by milliners of the Armoury resembles Russian bone-lace with rounded indents. The ornamentation is conspicuous for its high art quality which is at the same time modest and strict. The ornamentation in pearls of Russian work was also transferred from the caftan of the Tsar Ivan Alexeevich.

151. COACH OF PATRIARCH PHILARET. EARLY 17TH CENTURY. POLAND

Oak, birch, velvet, copper, iron. Gilding on gesso, wood-carving
Height 200 cm; length 550 cm; width 200 cm
Came from the Coach Court in 1834

The coach has no rotating sections, no springs and no coach-box. The rectangular body with understated doors is upholstered with cherry-coloured velvet; the copper nails that were used in the upholstering give it the form of square (a design typical for Poland in the 17th century). Each square is decorated with an eight-pointed star made of silver braid.
The six windows of the coach are made of mica sheets, the upper part of the doors have glass window panes which replaced the mica and were set in the 18th century. The front section and the upper cross-bar of the rear section are decorated with bronze slits and golden plates bearing the coat of arm of Poland and initials FLNKJB of the first possessor of this coach, Francisk Lesnowolski, the headman of Bryansk. The Patriarch Philaret (Feodor Nikitich Romanov, d. 1633) may have bought it from Lesnowolski when leaving Poland when he was in captivity during 1611-19.

According to another version, the coach was brought to Moscow in 1655 together with the other spoils of war during the Russian-Polish War. The great Russian painter V. I. Surikov (1846—1916) represented this coach in his picture "The Morning of the Strelitz Execution". The coach was in use till the late 17th century.

152. "KOLYMAGA" OF TSAR BORIS GODUNOV. LATE 16TH—EARLY 17TH CENTURY. ENGLAND

Oak, iron, leather straps, velvet. Woodcut, oil-painting
Height 250 cm; length 540 cm; width 230 cm
Came from the Coach Court before 1834
Presented to the Tsar Boris Godunov by the Queen Elisabeth Tudor of England (1533-1603) in 1603

The rectangular body of the "kolymaga" (coach) is placed between long wooden length-wise poles and fastened by broad leather straps upholstered with velvet. Instead of firm walls, windows and roof there is a canopy raised on eight small posts; the doors are replaced with the collapsible aprons. The armchairs in the coach are upholstered with Iranian velvet of the early 17th century, the walls are upholstered with Italian velvet. During the re-mounting in 1678 the coach was altered, so the walls, poles, wheels, the canopy's posts, a frame and a beam were decorated with wooden carvings. Besides, the coach was painted, its walls were embellished with pictures. The majority of historians in the 19th century date this coach to the late 16th century (i.e. N. I. Savvaitov, A. F. Weltmann, etc.). The carved scenes of battles between Christians and Moslems, as well as of the triumphant *démarche* of the victorious Christians, reflect the Russian-Turkish wars under the Tsar Boris Godunov's reign (1598—1605).
On ceremonial occasions the coach was used with a team of six or eight then fashionable. They were either led by the reins or by a coachman on one of the front horses.

153. EWER FOR HAND-WASHING ("VORONOK"). 1594-5. MADE BY JOHN MORLEY(?). LONDON, ENGLAND

Gilded silver. Chasing, carving, casting, repoussé, gilding
Height 33.5 cm
From the basic collection
Presented to the Tsar Mikhail Feodorovich (1596-1641) by the King of Denmark Christian IV in 1644

An ewer for rose water for hand-washing in early Russia was called the "voronok". As a rule, the ewer was brought with a special basin after meals. A form of the "voronok" appeared in England about 1555, at ceramic firstly, but to the late of the 16th century it became usual for the metal utensils. Thanks to the peculiarities of the vessel, it is possible to qualify it as a classical type of English "voronok". It draws attention with the simple magnificence and harmony of its graceful contours, with the connection of the decoration with form and material.

154. BASIN. LATE 16TH CENTURY. LONDON, ENGLAND

Gilded silver. Chasing, carving, gilding, puncheon
Diameter 40.7 cm; height 5.8 cm
From the basic collection
Supposed to be presented to the Tsar Mikhail Feodorovich by the English ambassador, Sir Thomas Smith, on December 21, 1613

From the numerous collection of English wash-basins, brought to Russia in the 16th and 17th centuries and indexed in the old archive documents, only two have been preserved in the Armoury. Both belong to the unknown craftsman with the unciphered monogram of the letters ∧V, vertically crossed, which is engraved in the little fancy shield.
Absolutely round, with clear-cut outlines, the basin is gilded and adorned with an ornament of concentric bands expanding from a prominence in the centre. The *repoussé* decorations are plane with deeply carved contours. Only bunches of fruit and sea-monsters on the brim of the basin are embossed in high relief. The ornament is smooth, shining, the background is punched. The decoration of the vessel does not resemble English silverware of the period. The pattern is stern in the English manner, but it is in harmony with the free lines of the drawing, and the strict accuracy of the lines is not contrary to the natural grace of the pattern.

155. SAKKOS OF PATRIARCH PARTHENIUS OF CONSTANTINOPLE. 1643. WEST-EUROPEAN EMBROIDERY

Spanish fabric
Brocaded satin
Length 142 cm; width (with sleeves) 142 cm
Came from the Patriarch Vestry
Brought to Moscow by the Greek Constantine Dmitriev on March 1659

Fabric and ornamentation of Spanish tissues of the 17th century are similar to the Italian ones of the same period. They distinguished both by an ornament in the shape of plant spouts, forming small marks, or, as it is in the present case, in the shape of parallel winding lines, small crowns and flowers in the places where they are joining. Though the design is compact, it is easy and exquisite. The deep-red field and the dead gold of the design embellish the décor most of all.
The front of the sakkos is embroidered with coloured silks and gold thread showing the Apostle Paul with three saints and the architectural constructions alternately. The collar is embroidered with gold thread with the words of a prayer and the year "1643".

156. EWER FOR HAND-WASHING. 1625 OR 1649. MADE BY CRAFTSMAN WITH MONOGRAM R.C. PARIS, FRANCE

Gilded silver. Casting, chasing, gilding
Height 35 cm
From the basic collection
Presented to the Alexei Mikhailovich (1625-76) by the King of the Great Britain Charles Stuart II in 1664

A silver gilded ewer from Paris, made by an unknown craftsman with the monogram R.C., is the adornment of the collection of French silverware kept in the Armoury. The beautiful logical forms of the vessel, its noble proportions, the ingenuous decorations could be created only by the skilful hand of a remarkable master. It is supposed to be made at the French Royal Manufacture, so it was naturally used later as a royal gift. The most outstanding and peculiar thing in the pompous ornamentations of the ewer is a combination of baroque forms with elements and methods of the former Renaissance style. The vessel is full of the graceful movement which is at the same time strong and impressive. Its impulses are seen everywhere: in the curved tendril of the handle, in the variety of disposition of Muses playing music, in the floating folds of their robes, in the twisted scrolls and "guttered" cartouches, in a dynamic line of the spout. But this movement is strict, it doesn't interfere with the whole of the decorated surface.

157. EWER. 1809-19. MADE BY JEAN BAPTISTE CLAUDE ODIOT (1763-1850). PARIS, FRANCE

Gilded silver. Casting, gilding, polishing, repoussé
Height 35 cm
Came from the Bufetnaya in the Winter Palace in 1921

The ewer by Jean B. Claude Odiot, intended for hot water, is interesting as a brilliant specimen of Empire style, at the same time it is characteristic of the individual manner of the artist.
Similar to many masterpieces of that style, the ewer though designed for everyday use, has an exquisite and luxurious form. Here again, as is usually found on the silver of Empire style, the entire gilding serves to display magnificence and splendour, just as the perfect polishing and the clear-cut contours, as well as the contrast of glittering and dead surfaces.
The ostentatious embellishments, as demanded by the style, are typical for Odiot: he liked rich plant ornaments and the application of large silver plates, often with figures of mythological personages.
The dead gold surface depicts a winged Eros on a hippocampus, masks of Satyr and Dionysus, a wreath of laurels on the handle, a garland of laurel leaves at the top, and a rosette of lotus leaves and flowers at the bottom.

158. SURPLICE. FRAGMENT. LATE 17TH—EARLY 18TH CENTURY. FRANCE

Silk. Hand-weaving
Length 139 cm; width 151 cm
Came from the Zlatoustovsky Monastery in 1924

The surplice is interwoven with broad vertical bands made of large bunches of leaves and flowers performed in a realistic manner. Little gold flowers with short straight stalks woven between the bands make the design calm and steady.
Contrast and harmony of the bright-green background with the bright silk and the golden pattern increase the splendour of this ornamental cloth. Various shades of silk render the colouring more luxurious and exquisite.

159. BASIN. 1625 OR 1649. MADE BY CRAFTSMAN WITH HALL-MARK "STALKING LION". PARIS, FRANCE

Gilded silver. Casting, chasing, engraving, gilding
Diameter 76 cm; height 73 cm
From the basic collection
Presented to the Tsar Alexei Mikhailovich by the King of the Great Britain Charles Stuart II in 1664

A luxurious wash-basin with corrugated brim and composition of numerous figures at the bottom is a rare but typical specimen of fancy utensils of the French court in the first half of the 17th century. It is easy to see the taste for pompous decorative designs, glorifying the absolute power of the king thanks to the artifices and splendour of the decoration, as well as to its pathetical theme. In the complicated scene depicting poem "La Gerusalemme Liberata" by Torquato Tasso (1544-95) the adopted baroque forms fall in with the traditional classical landscapes that are usually found in the background of those works. The exact proportions of the basin speaks for its classicism in which we can find a complexion of different styles so typical for the French masterpieces of the 17th century, even in this separate vessel as created in the country of the earliest European classicism.

160, 161, 162, 163. CEREMONIAL CAFTANS AND CAMISOLES OF EMPEROR PETER II. FIRST HALF 18TH CENTURY. FRANCE
Length 100 cm; width (is shoulders) 31.5 cm; width of hem 440 cm; length of sleeve 47 cm

CEREMONIAL CAFTAN AND CAMISOLE
Broadcloth, gold and silver thread. Embroidery

CEREMONIAL CAFTAN AND CAMISOLE
Caftan made of velvet; camisole made of brocade, gold and silver thread, embroidered

CEREMONIAL CAFTAN
Broadcloth, gold and silver thread. Embroidery

CEREMONIAL CAFTAN AND CAMISOLE
Caftan made of velvet; camisole made of silk brocade, gold and silver thread, embroidered
From the basic collection

Since the year 1700 outfits of Western cut became obligatory for Russian nobility. This new fashion ruined those who had to follow it; these new caftans and camisoles were exactly the opposite to the long heavy garments of the pre-Petrovian Russia, though they were neither superior in weight nor more comfortable. These Western coats matched the short pantaloons worn with long stockings and shoes; the powdered wigs that covered the heads and shoulders were the necessary accessories however hampering. The caftans and camisoles were made of luxurious and expensive fabrics as broadcloth, silk, brocade, usually of one colour. Skilful tailors embroidered them with gold and silver making floral and plant designs, as well as ornamented them even with gems and a great quantity of splendid buttons, so the pretentious embroidery became more gorgeous and expressive. The facets of wide bands of the luxurious embroidery bordered a flap, pockets, a collar and cuffs. The present caftans and camisoles come from the rich wardrobe of the Emperor Peter II (1715-30) who set the Western fashion in Russia. Most of his outfits were ordered in France. The caftans and camisoles of Peter II made of brocade, velvet and broadcloth are magnificently trimmed with gold and silver embroidery and buttons.

164. COACH OF EMPRESS ELIZAVETA PETROVNA. MID-18TH CENTURY. MADE BY BOURNIHALL. MINIATURES BY FRANÇOIS BOUCHER. PARIS, FRANCE

Maple, gold. Wood-carving, gilding on gesso, oil-painting
Height 270 cm; length 660 cm; width 250 cm
Came from the Coach Court in 1834
Presented to the Empress Elizaveta Petrovna by the Hetman of Ukraina K. G. Razumovsky (1728-1803)

The shape and decorations of the carriage are typical to rococo style. The gentle curves of its lines, the rich relief of carving, gilding and painting dominate over the general construction of the carriage. Curves, scrolls, sea-shells and all that remind the fluffy manes of the sea-horses or waves. The painting upon the carriage doors are made in pale-greys, pinks, blues and pale-blues usually found in the pictures of the great French painter Boucher (1703-70) in the last period of his creative work.
The carriage was made only for special occasions and seldom in use. Its enormous length and low body did not accommodate the bad long roads of Russia. The coach is in its original state: it has never been renovated.

165. DECORATIVE DISH. 1651-5. MADE BY MASTER WITH MONOGRAM N.T. AMSTERDAM, HOLLAND

Gilded silver. Chasing, repoussé, gilding
Diameter 78 cm; height 7 cm
Presented by the Dutch Embassy to the Tsar Alexei Mikhailovich in 1665

The dish was made at the time when the floral ornament was widely spread in Holland taking the place of the abstract one. So the festive silverware was adorned with the *repoussé* and engraved tulips, narcissi, peonies and carnations, so much admired in Holland. Just this combination of flowers is embossed in high relief on the bottom and the borders of the dish. The flowers, scrupulously worked in *repoussé*, are richly gilded, though the plane stalks with deepened outlines are faintly gilded, as well as the background. A fine nuancing of gilding together with the treatment of light and shade of the reliefs make the dish more picturesque. A combination of the European baroque with the individual ingenuousness of the Dutch floral style, as well as the irreproachable artistic manner renders the dishes real masterpiece.

RUSSIAN ART OF 18TH-19TH CENTURIES

166, 167. ARRAS. 1735. MADE IN TAPESTRY MANUFACTURE IN ST PETERSBURG

Length 276 cm; width 203 cm
Came from the Royal Palace in 1922
The inscription interwoven into its border reads: "Made in St Petersburg by Russian apprentices in 1735"

The arrases, a kind of rich tapestry with scenes and figures interwoven into it, usually pileless, hand-woven, were made in St Petersburg Manufacture during the years of 1717—1859. The manufacturing reached its high point in the second half of the 18th century when the producing of tapestries passed to national weavers.
The technique of tapestry without a pile was very complicated demanding from the craftsmen skill, artistic taste and much patience. The arrases were woven on the wrong side. The work had to be close to the pattern or coloured sample which was usually in the workshop. A little mirror that was placed below the web reflecting its right side had to help the weaver to compare his work with the correct standard; if there was no mirror, the weaver had to pass to the reverse side of the immense work and correct it from the right. The artist who had to choose colour, structure and quality of fibres was a weaver himself. In the largest of these tapestries with very complicated scenes more than 14,000 hues of wool and silk fibres were used. The greatest experts on these works could weave no more than one square meter during one year. The arras was used only for decorating the palaces and sometimes the cathedrals.

168. CORONATION ROBE OF EMPRESS CATHERINE I. 1724. ST PETERSBURG

Silk. Silver embroidery
Length of skirt 100 cm; width of hem 420 cm; waist 98 cm
Made for the coronation of the Empress Catherine I in 1724

The coronation robe of Catherine the Great (1684—1727) was the first ceremonial woman dress of European cut made in Russia. According to the fashion of the period, it consists of a bodice with short sleeves, a wide farthingale and a very long train. The length of the train corresponded with the rank of nobility. F. Bergholtz, a gentleman of the Emperor Bed-Chamber, wrote that the train of the coronation robe of Catherine the Great was carried by five ladies-in-waiting. A large decorative design of leaves, flowers and stylized crowns makes the clear-cut impressive rapport. A rich design at the edges of the train and skirt forms the rich fluffy fringe. The ornamentation though preserving the same elements changes in size from the edges and becomes smaller further in.

169. WEDDING GOWN OF EMPRESS CATHERINE II. 1745

Silver silk brocade, silver. Embroidery in silver
Length of skirt 107 cm; width of hem 578 cm; waist 46 cm
From the basic collection
Belonged to Catherine II (1729-96). Made for her wedding with the Crown-Prince of Russia Peter III (1728-62) in 1745

The wedding gown was made after the European fashion of the period. Rather uncomfortable for wear, such dresses quite corresponded with the magnificent rococo style and were in vogue till the late 18th century. A dress at those times was intended to make the person more conspicuous as an individual and show wealth and beauty. The costumes often were real works of art.

The wedding gown of Catherine II is remarkable for its wonderful embroidery. An embroidered pattern on the skirt and the bodice stresses a cut of the dress. A broad vertical band of large bunches of stylized flowers with stalks and leaves embroidered from the hem of the skirt towards the waist harmonizes with the numerous folds. The train (or the "tail", as it was called sometimes) fixed to the waist is ornamented with a narrow band of garlands with the same pattern.

170. SNUFF-BOX. 1780. MADE BY GEORGE ADOR (1724-84) MINIATURE MADE BY CORNELIUS GEYER. ST PETERSBURG

Gold, opal, enamel
Diameter 8.5 cm; height 1.9 cm
Came from the Royal Palace

The snuff-box is one of the latest masterpieces of George Ador made in the strict style of Classicism; it qualifies the jeweller as a first-class master with a deep knowledge of proportions, colouring and material.

The lid of the snuff-box bears a miniature portrait of Catherine II made by Danish painter Cornelius Geyer who had lived and worked in Russia during several years. The snuff-box is bordered with a fine setting stressing the form and the colouring of the miniature.

The lateral sides and the bottom of the snuff-box are entirely covered with grey-green enamel with reddish dots upon.

171. SNUFF-BOX. 1764. MADE BY GEORGE ADOR. ST PETERSBURG

Gold, brilliants. Carving, "kanfarenye", pictorial enamel
Length 2.5 cm; width 6.4 cm; height 2.5 cm
Came from Moscow Jewelry Association in 1926

The snuff-box is made by the best jeweller of the Russian Imperial Court at St Petersburg George Ador, Swiss-born, during the years of 1760s—80s. Exquisite and simple forms, fine and strict décor turn this snuff-box into a perfect specimen of the Classicism style in Russia and give it the worthy place among the masterpieces of well-known jewellers in West Europe. The brilliant monogram of the Empress Elizaveta Petrovna stands out in strong relief against the granulated background of the oval medallion, the compositional importance of which is stressed by gold of another colour and the polished surface of the lid. On the inner side of the lid is placed the enamelled portrait of the Empress.

172. PANAGIA. 1767

Silver, gold, brilliants, pictorial enamel
Height 16.5 cm; width 10 cm
Made to order of Catherine II
Came from the Cathedral of St Sophia in Novgorod in 1926

The panagia is a usual specimen of the pectoral plates of high priesthood in the middle and second half of the 18th century. Embellished with jewels, panagias resembled rather decorations or gorgeous jewelries.

This panagia was presented by the Empress Catherine II in 1767 to the Metropolitan Demetrius of Novgorod (1762-7). An oval medallion with the enamelled composition "The Coronation of the Virgin" is placed at the centre of the panagia. It is framed by a rich open-worked wreath, besprent entirely with brilliants of various size. The reverse side is decorated with the enamelled portrait of Catherine II surrounded with the carved presentation inscription which was usual for the presented panagias.

173. PHELONION. 1770. EMBROIDERED BY DARYA LIKHNOVSKAYA. ST PETERSBURG

Ornamentation in pearls of Russian work
Velvet, pearls, gems. Hand-weaving
Length 141 cm
Came from the Zagorsk Museum of History and Fine Arts in 1928
Presented by Catherine II to the Moscow Metropolitan Platon (1787-1812)

The design of the phelonion made in oblique checks is formed by thin pearl branches and is filled with an ornament of a rose-branch and a bunch of grapes by turn; in whole it repeats the pattern of precious fabrics fashionable at that time. The phelonion is embroidered with pearls of various size. High technique and beautiful décor show the skill and artistic taste of the gold-milliner Darya Likhnovskaya who had embroidered the phelonion very scrupulously during the two years. The phelonion is embroidered with more than 150 hundred of pearls. At the same time some articles of ecclesiastical vestments were embroidered to be a present of Catherine II to the Trinity-Sergius Monastery.

The pearls for these purposes were ripped off from early clothes and icons.

174. CORONATION ROBES. 19TH CENTURY

Silver silk brocade. Embroidery
Robe of the Empress Alexandra Feodorovna, wife of the Emperor Nicholas I (1796-1825 (in foreground)

The coronation robes of the Russian empresses usually had a cut in the fashion of the time, but according to the traditions settled in the mid-19th century they were made from silver silk brocade and decorated with embroidery, spangles and thin lace.

At the first quarter of the 19th century the coronation robes were almost straight, with a high waist fluffy short sleeves and a long train fixing to the bodice.

175. INTERIOR OF COACH HALL

To the left

HOODED SLEDGE OF EMPRESS ELIZAVETA PETROVNA. 1741. ST PETERSBURG

Oak, birch, iron, broadcloth. Carving, oil-painting
Height 200 cm; length 600 cm; width 200 cm
Comes from the Coach Court in 1834

In the centre

COACH OF EMPRESS ELIZAVETA PETROVNA OF COUPÉ TYPE. 1740. WIENNA, AUSTRIA

Ash-tree, iron, copper. Gilding on gesso, oil-painting, carving
Height 255 cm; length 500 cm; width 200 cm
Comes from the Coach Court in 1834

To the right

COACH OF PRINCE FREDERIC OF HOLSTEIN. 1721. FRANCE

Oak, iron. Gilding on gesso, oil-painting, carving
Height 245 cm; length 550 cm; width 210 cm
Comes from the Coach Court in 1834

The construction of the coach of the Empress Elizaveta Petrovna (1709-61) is usual for the winter coaches of the 17th and 18th centuries. The coach has four doors and ten windows, with an elongated table and braziers in the centre and narrow benches upholstered in green cloth lining the sides of the coach. The body of the coach is decorated with carving, gilding, oil-painting. Carved large cartouches supported by eagles bearing the initials of the Empress are placed on the front and back walls. Such winter sledges (the so-called "lineya") were intended for winter journeys of high nobility. The body of the Austrian carriage is suspended on straps and has metal cranked springs, rotating front sections, a "swan-neck", etc. The coach was in use till the very mid-19th century. No considerable alterations were done.

BIOGRAPHICAL NOTES

A B B A S I (1557—1628), Shah of Persia (1587—1628) of the Safavid dynasty; guarded the interests of the feudal lords and rich merchants; outstanding army leader

A B B A S I I, Shah of Persia during the second half of the seventeenth century. Friendly towards Russia. In 1664 granted immunity and privileges to Russian merchants and free trade rights in all Persian cities

A D O R, G E O R G E S (1724—84), Swiss-born jeweller to the Russian Imperial Court at St Petersburg; came to Russia about 1764, where he died in 1784

A D R I A N, Patriarch of All Russia (1690—1700)

A L E X I U S (exact date of birth unknown, probably between 1292 and 1298, died 1378), Metropolitan of Kiev and All Russia from 1354, of the family of Moscow Boyards Plescheyevs. Guardian of the infant Prince Dmitri Donskoi and in that capacity the factual head of government. Worked to strengthen the Moscow princedom

A L E X E I M I K H A I L O V I C H (1629—76), Russian tsar from 1645, second tsar of the Romanov dynasty; the son of Mikhail Feodorovich and Yevdokia Streshneva

A L E X E I P E T R O V I C H (1690—1718), Tsarevich, eldest son of Peter the Great and Yevdokia Lopukhina

A L F E R Y E V, O S I P, an armourer. Worked in the Armoury in the middle of the seventeenth century

A N D R O N O V, outstanding Russian master armourer in the first half of the seventeenth century

A N N A V A S S I L I E V N A, daughter of Prince Vassili I of Moscow and Sophia Witowtovna

A N T H O N Y, Metropolitan of Moscow, 1577—80

A N T R O P O V, A L E X E I P E T R O V I C H (1716—1765), well-known Russian portrait painter. In 1761 appointed chief supervisor of icon painting and other works for the Synod

A R D I T I, A N D R E A, Italian goldsmith, worked in Florence in the middle of the fourteenth century

B A T O R Y, S T E P H E N (1533—86), King of Poland from 1576. Conducted anti-Russian policy

B O R I S A L E X A N D R O V I C H, Grand Prince of Tver from 1425 to 1461, aspired to the title of Prince of All Russia

B O R I S G O D U N O V (c. 1551—1605), Boyard and factual ruler during the reign of Feodor Ivanovich, who was married to Godunov's sister Irina. Tsar between 1598 and 1605. Clever, well-educated, ambitious. a shrewd politician

B O U C H E R, F R A N Ç O I S (1703—70), French painter and engraver, major exponent of Rococo style

B O U R N I H A L L, French saddler and coach maker in the middle of the eighteenth century

B U C K E N D A L E, J O H N, English saddler and coach maker in the middle of the eighteenth century

C A T H E R I N E I, A L E X E Y E V N A (1684—1727), Empress of All Russia (1725—1727)

C A T H E R I N E I I, A L E X E Y E V N A (1729—96), Empress of All Russia from 1762, b. Princess of Anhalt-Zerbst

C H A R L E S I I (1630—85), King of Great Britain and Ireland

C H A R L E S X I I (1682—1718), King of Sweden from 1697. In 1709 defeated by the Russian army in the Battle of Poltava

C H R I S T I A N I V (1588—1649), King of Denmark. During 1630s war against Sweden tried unsuccessfully to draw Russia into the anti-Swedish coalition

C O M N E N I, dynasty of Byzantine Emperors (1057—1185), except for the period 1059—81

C O N S T A N T I N U S I, Constantine the Great (b. 274 A. D.). Emperor of Rome 306—337, sole ruler of both E. and W. Empires. Between 326 and 330 transferred his capital from Rome to Byzantium. Large scale construction and fresco painting in secular and church buildings in Novgorod and other towns of Novgorod land are connected with his name

F E O D O R A L E X E Y E V I C H (1661—82), Russian tsar, 1676—82, son of the Tsar Alexei Mikhailovich and his first wife, M. P. Miloslavskaya

F E O D O R I V A N O V I C H (1557—98), Russian tsar from 1584, son of the Tsar Ivan the Terrible. The last of the Rurik dynasty

F I L I M O N O V, G E O R G I D M I T R I E V I C H (1828—98), Russian archeologist and art historian. From 1858 F. was in charge of the archives and office of the Armoury. Main works: "Simon Ushakov and Russian Icon Painting of His Time" and "The Index of Hallmarks on Armoury Silver" (M., 1893)

F R O B O S, Y U R I V I L I M O V, Russian goldsmith and jeweller during second half of the seventeenth century

G E Y E R, C O R N E L I U S, Dutch painter. Lived in Russia between 1781 and 1783, and 1797 and 1798

G O L I T S Y N, V A S S I L I V A S S I L I E V I C H (1643—1714), Prince, army leader and statesman, one of the most educated men of his time. As the favourite of Tsarevna Sophia was the factual head of the state between 1682 and 1689. After the revolt of 1689 which brought Peter the Great to power he was arrested and banished to Archangel Province, where he lived until his death

G R I G O R I E V, S P I R I D O N, icon painter working from 1671 at the Armoury. A pupil of Feodor Yelizariev, chief painter at Patriarch Chamber

G R Y A Z E V, I V A N K I R I L L O V I C H (d. 1634), Clerk of Land Office in 1621, worked at the Russian Embassy in Denmark in 1631 and on return home was made an official at the Royal Duma

H O P E N H A U P T, J O H A N N (1709—53), German coach maker, born in Merseburg. In 1747 worked for the Berlin court and did some interior decoration for Sans-Souci

I R I N A F E O D O R O V N A G O D U N O V A (d. 1603), Russian Tsarina, sister of Boris Godunov, wife of Tsar Feodor Ivanovich. After husband's death in 1598 took the veil at Novodevichy Convent and became known as the Nun Alexandra

I V A N I, D A N I L O V I C H, K A L I T A (d. 1340), Prince of Moscow from 1325, Grand Prince of Moscow from 1328. Enlarged the territory of the Moscow princedom and strengthened the importance of Moscow. His nickname "Kalita" means "Moneybags"

I V A N I I I, V A S S I L I E V I C H (1440—1505), Grand Prince of Moscow from 1462, prominent statesman who united the majority of Russian lands into one state. Established relations with the See of Rome and with Germany, Hungary, Turkey, Persia and other countries. Built the modern walls and towers of the Moscow Kremlin as well as the Cathedrals of the Dormition 1475—79 and of the Annunciation 1484—89, Granovitaya Palata (Faceted Palace) 1487—91, and started building the Cathedral of the Archangel Michael in 1505.

IVAN IV, VASSILIEVICH, THE TERRIBLE (1530—84), from 1533 the Grand Prince, and from 1547 the Tsar and Grand Prince of All Russia. First Russian Tsar and a major political figure

IVAN V, ALEXEYEVICH (1666—96), son of Tsar Alexei Mikhailovich by his first wife M. I. Miloslavskaya. Reigned from 1682 as the "first" tsar (his brother Peter the Great was at that time counted the "second" tsar), subservient to the will of his sister Tsarevna Sophia

IVAN IVANOVICH (d. 1364), Prince of Zvenigorod, younger brother of Dmitri Donskoi

IVAN IVANOVICH (1554—1581), elder son of Ivan the Terrible, murdered by his father in 1581

IVANOV, MAXIM, painter at the Armoury during the latter half of the seventeenth century

JOACHIM (1620—90), ninth and penultimate Patriarch of All Russia, from 1674, of the family of Mozhaisk noblemen Savelov. Author of pamphlets against dissidents in the Russian church

JOASAPH II, Patriarch of All Russia from 1667 to 1673

JOB, Metropolitan of All Russia 1586—89; Patriarch of Moscow and All Russia from February 26, 1589 to 1605

JOHN III, PALEOLOGOS, Byzantine Emperor from 1425 to 1448

JOHN AUTORIANUS, State Secretary (1059—61) to Constantine Ducas, Emperor of Byzantium

JONAS, Metropolitan of Moscow and All Russia from 1433, formerly Bishop of Ryazan. Canonized in seventeenth century

JAMES I (1565—1625), King of England 1603—25, son of Mary, Queen of Scots

KHITROVO, BOGDAN (JOB) MATVEYEVICH (c. 1615—1680), boyard, palace steward and courtier closest to Tsar Alexei Mikhailovich

KOBENTZEL, HANS, Ambassador of the German Emperor Maximilian II to Russia during the second half of the sixteenth century

KOSHKA, FEODOR ALEXEYEVICH, Moscow Boyard, adviser to Dmitri Donskoi and his son Vassili. In 1380 when Dmitri Donskoi set out to fight the Tartar Khan Mamai, K. was left in charge of Moscow

KRAMER, TOBIAS, German goldsmith who worked in Augsburg in 1615—34

LIKHNOVSKAYA, DARYA, gold thread embroiderer at St Petersburg Court during the latter half of the eighteenth century

LUCIAN, Russian goldsmith at the beginning of the fifteenth century

MACKENZON, ANDREAS, seventeenth century German master silversmith

MANUEL II, PALEOLOGOS, Emperor of Byzantium, 1391—1425

MARIA TEMRYUKOVNA (d. 1569), Princess Kuchenei, daughter of Temryuk Andarovich, Prince of Kabardah. From 1562 Tsarina of Russia, second wife of Tsar Ivan the Terrible

MATVEEV, ARTAMON SERGEYEVICH (1625—82), famous Russian diplomat. Held the view that the Ukraine must join Russia. Enjoyed great influence in state affairs during the reign of Tsar Alexei Mikhailovich

MAXIMOV, IVAN, painter at the Armoury during the latter half of the seventeenth century

MIKHAIL FEODOROVICH (1596—1645), Russian tsar from 1613, first of the Romanov dynasty. Son of Boyard Feodor Nikitich who later became Patriarch Philaret. Played no independent role as a statesman

MIKHAILOV, KONON, famous armourer at the Armoury during the first half of the seventeenth century

MININ, KOZMA (Kuzma Minich Zakharyev-Sukhoruk), died 1616. One of the chief organizers and leaders of the liberation fight against the Polish invaders in 1611—12. Governor of Nizhni-Novgorod and meat merchant

MORLEY, JOHN, seventeenth century English jeweller

MOROZOV, BORIS IVANOVICH (1590—1661), nobleman and tutor of Tsar Alexei Mikhailovich. The factual ruler of Russia in 1645—8. One of the biggest landowners

MOROZOVA, ANNA ILYINICHNA, Boyard, sister of Tsarina Maria Ilyinichna, who was the wife of Tsar Alexei Mikhailovich. Was married to Boyard Boris Ivanovich Morozov

MORES DER ÄLTESTE, JACOB (d. between 1610 and 1612), silversmith to the Imperial House of Hapsburg. Mentioned in documents of 1579

MOSES, Archbishop of Novgorod during the first half of the fourteenth century

MSTISLAVSKY, FEODOR IVANOVICH (d. 1622), Prince, head of the Boyard government 1610—11. Army leader during the war against Sweden in 1590—3

MUMIN-MOHAMMED, sixteenth century Persian craftsman, master of inlaid work

NARYSHKINA, NATALIA KIRILLOVNA (1652—94), mother of Peter the Great, second wife of Tsar Alexei Mikhailovich

NICHOLAS I (1796—1855), Russian Emperor from 1825

NICON (Nikita Minov), 1605—81, Patriarch, prominent church and state leader. Strove to strengthen the position of the church to give it precedence in state affairs

NIKITIN, PAVEL, painter at the Armoury during the second half of the seventeenth century

NIZAMI OF GANJA, ILYAS BIN YUSUF-OGLY (born c. 1141, died c. 1203), great Azerbaijanian poet and thinker. Chief works: "Khamsé", "Khosrau and Shirin," "Leilah and Mejnun," and "Iskandar-nama"

ODIOT, Jean Baptiste Claude (1763—1850), French jeweller

OLENIN, ALEXEI NIKOLAYEVICH (1763—1843), Russian archeologist, historian, painter and senior civil servant. From 1817 President of the Academy of Fine Arts in St Petersburg

PALEOLOGOS, last dynasty of the Byzantine emperors, which ruled from 1261 to 1453

PESTRIKOV, TRETYAK, gold and silversmith during the first half of the seventeenth century

PETER, first Metropolitan of Moscow and All Russia (1308—26); the ally of Ivan Kalita during the struggle between the appanage princedoms. Transferred the seat of the Russian church from Vladimir to Moscow, thus adding to the political importance of Moscow princedom. Began the construction of the Dormition Cathedral at the Moscow Kremlin. Peter was canonized in 1339

PETER I, THE GREAT (1671—1725), Tsar of Russia from 1682 and from 1721 the Emperor; an outstanding statesman and army leader

PETER II (1715—30), Russian Emperor, 1727—30. Grandson of Peter the Great, son of Tsarevich Alexei Petrovich and Princess Sophia Charlotta of Blankenburg

PETER III (1728—62), Russian Emperor, 1761—2

PHILARET (Feodor Nikitich Romanov), d. 1663, Patriarch of Moscow and All Russia, 1619—33. A prominent Boyard, he was a first cousin of the Tsar Feodor Ivanovich. In 1601 was forced to take monastic vows. One time a Polish prisoner, on his release in

1619 Philaret was appointed Patriarch and received the title of "Grand Seigneur" and reigned together with his son, Tsar Mikhail Feodorovich

PHILOTHEUS KOKKIN (d. 1379), Patriarch of Constantinople who held the office twice, 1354—5 and 1362—76. Philotheus was a well-educated person and a writer

PHOTIUS, Metropolitan of Moscow (1409—31), b. in Monemvasia, Greece. On September 2, 1408, was appointed Metropolitan of Kiev and All Russia; arrived at Kiev on September 1, 1409, and in spring 1410 left for Moscow

PITIRIM, Patriarch of All Russia, 1672—3

PICCININO, LUCIO. of Milan. Italian goldsmith. Mentioned in documents for 1550—1600

PLATON. Metropolitan of Moscow, 1787—1811

POGODIN, Mikhail Petrovich (1800—75), Russian historian and writer

POPOV, Ivan. silversmith at the Gold and Silver Halls of the Moscow Kremlin during the first half of the seventeenth century

POSIER (1716—64), Swiss-born jeweller at the Court at St Petersburg

POTAPOV, MAKAR, painter at the Armoury during the latter half of the seventeenth century

POZHARSKY, DMITRI MIKHAILOVICH (1578?—1642?), Prince, outstanding Russian army leader and political figure who with K. Minin headed the struggle against the Polish-Swedish intervention of 1608—12

RAZUMOVSKY, KIRILL GRIGORIEVICH (1728—1808), the last Hetman of the Ukraine from 1750, President of the Academy of Sciences at St Petersburg 1745—65; Field Marshal from 1764

RUBLEV, ANDREI (c. 1370—1430), great Russian icon painter

SAFI, Shah of Persia, first half of the seventeenth century

SAPIEHA, LEO, Polish Ambassador to Russia, end of sixteenth-early seventeenth century. In 1600 negotiated on behalf of King Sigismund III Vasa a union between Poland and Russia

SIGISMUND III, VASA (1566—1632), King of Poland, 1587—1632 and King of Sweden, 1592—1604. His election as King was hoped to promote the Polish-Swedish union against Russia. During his reign Polish troops invaded Russia, 1604—18

SIMON, Metropolitan of Moscow, 1496—1519

SOLOVIEV, SERGEI MIKHAILOVICH (1802—79), prominent Russian historian

SOPHIA WITOWTOVNA (died c. 1451), daughter of Grand Prince Witowt of Lithuania, married Grand Prince Vassili Dmitrievich of Moscow (1371—1453) in 1390

SOPHIA PALEOLOGOS (d. 1503), daughter of Thomas Paleologos, brother of Byzantine Emperor Constantine. Became second wife of Grand Prince Ivan III of Moscow in 1472; marriage greatly influenced the form of Moscow rule and all external signs of state power

STRESHNEV, VASSILI IVANOVICH, Boyard and high officer of state, was in charge of the Armoury and Gold and Silver Halls from 1630 to 1638. Between 1634 and 1645 was entrusted with various diplomatic assignments

STROGANOV, GEORGY DMITRIEVICH (1656—1715), famous merchant and businessman who sent two fully equipped frigates at his own expense to fight in the Northern War of 1711. He had 44,643 serfs, besides 33,235 "who had escaped and are wandering." In his capacity as first-rank citizen, S. could build towns and fortresses, maintain a private army and fight against Siberian khanates, and trade tax-free. Peter the Great conferred the rank of baron on Stroganov's sons

TASSO. TORQUATO (1544—1595), famous Italian Renaissance poet. Two of his poems "La Gerusalemme Liberata" (1580) and "La Gerusalemme Conquistata" (1593) provided subject matter for a number of works of art during the era of classicism

TERENTIEV, DMITRI, gem cutter at the Gold Hall during the last quarter of the seventeenth century

TITOV, VASSILI (d. 1681), famous armourer. Worked at the Armoury from 1650

TON, KONSTANTIN ANDREYEVICH (1794—1881). Russian architect, the chief exponent of the official pseudo-Russian style of 1830—1850s. Built the Armoury (1851) and the Grand Palace (1838—49) in the Moscow Kremlin

TRETYAKOV, PYOTR ALEXEYEVICH (d. 1618), Duma secretary who held high posts at the Land and Foreign Offices

USHAKOV, SIMON (or Pimen), 1625—86, famous icon painter who worked in the Armoury

VASSILI I, DMITRIEVICH (1371—1425), Grand Prince of Moscow from 1389, eldest son of Dmitri Donskoi. Added Suzdal, Nizhny-Novgorod, Murom and Tarussa provinces to Moscow princedom. During his reign Moscow began to acquire the features of the cultural centre of all Russia. Was married to Sophia, daughter of the Grand Prince Witowt of Lithuania

VASSILI II, THE BLIND (1415—62), Grand Prince of Moscow from 1425, grandson of Dmitri Donskoi

VASSILI III, IVANOVICH (1478—1533), Grand Prince of Moscow from 1505, son of Ivan III and Sophia Paleologos. In his regin the unification of the Russian lands around Moscow was completed

VASSILIEV, MIKHAIL, master craftsman in the Gold Hall in the last quarter of the seventeenth century

VASSILIEV, SERGEI, painter at the Armoury in the latter half of the seventeenth century

VSEVOLOD THE GREAT NEST (1154—1212), son of Yuri Dolgoruki. From 1176 Grand Prince of Vladimir, was the most powerful Russian prince of the time. Vladimir-Suzdal Princedom reached its cultural zenith during his reign. Had twelve children, hence the nickname "Great Nest"

VYATKIN, GRIGORI, an armourer. Mentioned in various documents between 1649 and 1688. Master craftsman in the Armoury who made barrels, matchlocks and flintlocks for firearms

YAKOVLEV, MIKHAIL, master craftsman at the Patriarch's Gold Hall of the Moscow Kremlin during the latter half of the seventeenth century

YAROSLAV VSEVOLODOVICH (1191—1246), Prince of Pereslavl-Zalessky, father of Alexander Nevsky

YEGOTOV, IVAN VASSILIEVICH (1756—1815), Russian architect of classical style, designer of the old 1810 Armoury Building

YERMAK TIMOFEYEVICH (d. 1584), Cossack hetman. Famous for conquest of Siberia. Added Western Siberia to Russian state as a result of military campaigns of 1581—1584

YURI VSEVOLODOVICH (c. 1187—1238), Grand Prince of Vladimir from 1212

YURI DOLGORUKY (c. 1090—1157), Prince of Rostov and Suzdal, and later Grand Prince of Kiev. Founded the city of Moscow. Yuri was the son of Vladimir Monomachos

YURIEV, AVRAAM, Russian goldsmith at the Armoury in first half of the seventeenth century

YURIEV, FEODOR, painter at the Armoury in second half of the seventeenth century

ZABELIN, IVAN YEGOROVICH (1820—1909), Russian historian and archeologist

ZUBOV, FEODOR YEVSTIKHIEV, painter at the Armoury during the latter half of the seventeenth century

G L O S S A R Y

Altabas, a kind of brocade made of wire-drawn gold or silver. Very thick, rigid

"Baidana" (from Arabian "badan"), a short defensive coat of mail made of large damascened rings

"Bakhterets", a defensive coat of mail made of small plaques instead of rings

"Basma", hand-stamping of various designs on different materials, on the thinnest gold or silver plaques in particular

"Barmy" (from Greek "barmy", «burden»), a necklace, broad collar or yoke worn over luxurious garments of Grand Princes

"Bratina", a ball-shaped vessel for drinking, usually metal

Cabochon, any precious stone cut in convex shape, polished but not faceted

Cameo, a gem having two layers with an image carved on one layer so that it raises on the background of the other. Known since 4th century B.C.

Censer, an ornamented container suspended on chains in which incense is burned

Ceremonial horse, a horse in precious trappings used on festive occasions

"Chaldar", a horse-cloth covering a horse's front, sides and croup

Chalice, the cup for wine of Holy Communion

"Charka", a small cup for wine with a small flat handle

Church Feasts, legends glorifying Christ and the Virgin

Damask, a reversible fabric, usually of silk or linen, in figured weave

Damask steel, steel decorated with wavy lines or inlaid gold and silver, originally made in Damascus and used for sword blades. Called "red" or "blue", subject to its colour

Deesis, ecclesiastical composition with Christ surrounded by St. John the Forerunner and the Virgin. The composition also represents the Archangels Michael and Gabriel, the Apostles Peter and Paul and other saints. The images are disposed in strict order

Enamel, a glassy, coloured opaque substance. Powdered and diluted with water, it is fused to surfaces of metals. Ground and polished, the substance turned to a shining steady-coloured film. Subject to the technique of enamel superposition and fixing on metal, there are *champlevé*, *cloisonné*, painted, glazed, transparent and opaque enamels

"Endova", a large roundish drinking vessel for mead, beer, kvass, with a spout. Resembles a "bratina"

Filigree, delicate lacelike ornamental work of intertwined wire of gold, silver, etc.

Filigree gold, a silk or flax thread intertwined with silver wrei often gilded

Gold or silver thread, a silk or flax thread winding round the finest silver wire, often gilded

Granulation, a technique of decorating objects in precious metal by soldering small grains of gold or silver on them

Hoofed pattern, a pattern in the shape of a hole or a hoof. Used in Iranian, Turkish and Bokharan fabrics

Hexamite, precious fabric, fleecy or pileless, patterned; 5 fibres of warp; interwoven with twisted gold or silver on the silk background. The best hexamites were made in Venetia. Five metres of hexamite weigh 16kg

Looped hexamite is woven of thick golden threads forming large loops;

Hexamited velvet is the highest sort of velvet, patterned with woven loops of gold and silver threads

Inlay, a design or pattern made by inlaying. Inlaying is done by cutting patterns and designs on the surface of wood, etc. and filling the spaces with other kinds of wood, or with metal, ivory, etc.

"Kanfarenye", a special technique of chasing made by a puncheon ("kanfar") in the shape of a blunt needle or with a small ring at the end. The background made in this technique in early Russia was called "kanfarenny", i.e. ornamented with small roundels or dots

"Khoz", specially treated goat-skin; variously coloured

"Kindek", thin cotton fabric

"Namiot", a horse-cloth covering the saddle

"Nauz", a precious tassel made of gold and silver threads and pearls; put on the horse's neck as an amulet and (in 16th-17th century) as a decoration

Niello, any of a number of alloys of sulfur with silver, lead, copper, etc., characterized by deep-black colour and used to decorate objects of other methods by means of inlay

Orphrey, a rich decorative metal plate placed on the front of some ecclesiastical robes

Panagia (from Greek "pan-agia" that means "all sacred"), a pectoral icon of high priesthood

Panne, silk or half-silk fabric resembling velvet but having a longer nap that makes the pattern raised

Paten, a round plate holding bread in the Eucharist

Phelonion, a sleeveless wide outer vestment, long from behind and short at the front; worn over the surplice by priests

"Pokrovets", a small rectangular piece of precious fabric put on the saddle of the ceremonial horse

"Saadak" (or "sagadak"), a bow with a bow case and a quiver for arrows. Richly decorated

Sakkos, a vestment of patriarchs and metropolitans; a straight long tunic with short wide sleeves and a round collar

Sceptre, a rod or staff, highly ornamented, held by rulers on ceremonial occasions as a symbol of authority and sovereignty

Shabrack, a horse-cloth covering the horse's croup. Made of rich fabric, embroidered and decorated with gems

Shrine, a case or other container holding sacred relics, as the bone of a saint

Shroud, an icon embroidered on the piece of cloth in silk, gold or silver threads

Shroud of Christ, a cut-off piece of cloth embroidered with "The Entombment"

Staurothèque, a container holding sacred relics, in the shape of a square wooden box with a lid faced with silver. Inwards, a hollow where the cross is

Stole, a long decorated strip of cloth with crosses, worn like a scarf by officiating clergymen

"Stopa", a high tankard. In late 17th century, a glass on the stand

Surplice, a loose, wide-sleeved cloak or gown worn variously, over the cassock, by clergy and choir

Zion, a representation of the Cathedral of the Redeemer on Mount Zion which in ecclesiastical usage was a symbol of the Church. The Zions were only in chief cathedrals of Kiev, Novgorod, Pskov, Vladimir and Moscow

Tinsel, thin sheets, strips or threads of gold used for inexpensive decoration

"Voronok", a ewer with a spherical body and a cylindrical neck

"Zvezdnitsa", a church ware in the shape of four metal arches linked upwards. Stood on the paten

B I B L I O G R A P H Y

А д е л у н г Ф. Критико-литературное обозрение путешественников по России до 1700 года. М., 1864

А р с е н ь е в Ю. В. и Т р у т о в с к и й В. К. «Оружейная палата». Путеводитель, изд. 4-е. М., 1914

А р т а м о н о в М. И. Эрмитаж. Л., «Советский художник», 1964

Б а н к А. В. Византийское искусство в собраниях Советского Союза. М.—Л., «Советский художник», 1967

Б а з е л е в и ч К. В. Имущество московских князей в XIV—XV вв.— В кн. «Труды ГИМ», вып. 3. М., 1926

Б а к л а н о в а Н. А. Привозные товары в Московском государстве во второй половине XVII в. Труды ГИМ, вып. 4, 1928

Б а р т е н е в С. Московский Кремль в старину и теперь, ч. I и II. М., 1916

Б а х р у ш и н С. В. Научные труды. I. Очерки по истории ремесла, торговли и городов русского централизованного государства XVI — начала XVII веков. М., изд-во Академии наук СССР, 1952

B a u e r J. A., H. J e l i n e k. Edelelsteine. Artia. 1966

В е л ь т м а н А. Московская Оружейная палата. М., 1860

В и к т о р о в А. Е. Описание записных книг и бумаг старинных дворцовых приказов (1584—1725), вып. 1—2. М., 1877—1882

В и с к о в а т о в А. Историческое описание одежды и вооружения русских войск, 1841

Г е р б е р ш т е й н С и г и з м у н д. Записки о московитских делах. СПб., Суворин, 1908

Г и л я р о в с к а я Н. Русский исторический костюм для сцены. М.—Л., «Искусство», 1945.

Г о л ь д б е р г Т. Г. и П о с т н и к о в а - Л о с е в а М. М. Клеймение серебряных изделий в XVII—XVIII вв. (К истории серебряного дела в России).— В изд. «Труды Государственного Исторического музея», вып. XVIII. М., 1947

Г о л ь д б е р г Т. Г. Черневое серебро Великого Устюга. М., 1952

Г о р с е й Д ж е р о м. Записки о Московии XVI в. СПб., 1905

«Государственная Оружейная палата Московского Кремля». Альбом. М., 1958

«Государственная Оружейная палата Московского Кремля». Сборник научных статей. М., «Искусство», 1954

Г о т ь е Ю. В. Английские путешественники в Московском государстве в XVI в. М., 1937

Д е н и с о в а М. М., П о р т н о в М. Э. Тульское художественное оружие XVIII—XIX вв. М., Госкультпросвет, 1952

Д и н ц е с А. А. Мотив Московского герба в народном искусстве.— В кн. «Сообщения Государственного Русского музея», вып. 2. Л., 1947, стр. 30—33

З а б е л и н И. Е. Домашний быт русских царей в XVI—XVII столетиях, ч. I—II. М., 1915—1918

З а б е л и н И. Е. Домашний быт русских цариц в XVI—XVII столетиях, изд. 3. М., 1901

З а б е л и н И. Е. История русской жизни с древнейших времен. М., 1912

З а б е л и н И. Е. Историческое обозрение финифтяного и ценинного дела в России.— «Записки имп. Археологического о-ва», т. VI, 1833

З а б е л и н И. Е. О металлическом производстве в России до конца XVII в.— «Записки имп. Археологического о-ва», т. V, 1853

Именное и художественное холодное оружие XVII—XIX веков. М., Госкультпросвет, 1956

«История Москвы», тт. 1—2. М., изд-во Академии наук СССР, 1953

«История русского искусства», тт. 1—8. Изд-во Академии наук СССР, 1953—1964

J o n e s A. The Old English Plate of the Emperor of Russia. London

«Книга об избрании на царство царя и великого князя Михаила Федоровича». М., 1856

К о л о г р и в о в С. Н. Государева Большая шкатула.— «Вестник археологии и истории». СПб., 1903

К о л о г р и в о в С. Н. Материалы к истории сношений России с иностранными державами. СПб., 1911

К о р з у х и н а Г. Ф. Русские клады XI—XIII веков. М.— Л., изд-во Академии наук СССР, 1954

К о р ш Е. Русское серебряное дело и его орнаментация.— «Старые годы», 1909, июль — сентябрь

К о т о ш и х и н Г р и г о р и й. О России в царствование Алексея Михайловича, изд. 4. СПб., 1906

K r e i s e l H. Prunkwagen und Schlitten. 1927

Л е в и н с о н Н. В. Мастера — художники Москвы XVII в.— В кн. «Труды ГИМ». «Памятники культуры», вып. 31. М., 1961

Л е н ц Э. Указатель отделения средних веков и эпохи Возрождения. СПб., 1908

M a r t i n F. R. Dänische Silberschätze aus der Zeit Christians IV aufbewahrt in der kaiserlichen Schatzkammer zu Moskau. Stockholm. 1900

M a r t i n F. R. Schwedische königliche Geschenke an Russische Zaren. Stockholm. 1900

Н и к о л а е в а Т. В. Произведения мелкой пластики XIII—XVII вв. в собрании Загорского музея. 13-е изд.— Сообщения Загорского гос. историко-художественного музея-заповедника. Загорск, 1960

O m a n C h a r l e s. The English silver in the Kremlin 1557—1663. London. 1961

Опись домашнему имуществу царя Ивана Васильевича.— «Временник Московского общества истории и древностей Российских», 1850, кн. 7, отд. II, стр. 1—64

Опись Московской Оружейной палаты, ч. I—VII. М., 1884—1893

Оружейная палата Московского Кремля. М., изд-во «Московский рабочий», 1964

П а в е л А л е п п с к и й. Путешествие антиохийского патриарха Макария в Россию в половине XVII в., описанное его сыном архидьяконом Павлом Алеппским, вып. 1—5. М., «Об-во истории и древностей Российских», 1896—1900

П и с а р с к а я Л. В. «Византийское искусство V—XV вв.» Каталог. М.—Л., 1964

«По Кремлю». Путеводитель, 4-е изд. М., изд-во «Московский рабочий», 1967

Постникова-Лосева М. М. Русские серебряные и золотые ковши. М., Госкультпросветиздат, 1953

Постникова-Лосева М. М. и Платонова Н. Г. Русское художественное серебро. Труды ГИМ, вып. 28. М., «Советская Россия», 1959

Rosenberg M. Der Goldschmiede Merkzeichen. 1—4. Frankfurt M., Berlin. 1922—1928

Rosenberg M. Jamnitzer. Frankfurt M. 1920

«Русское декоративное искусство», т. 1—3. М., изд-во Академии художеств СССР, 1962—1965

Рыбаков Б. А. Ремесло Древней Руси. М., изд-во Академии наук СССР, 1948

Русская культура XVIII в. М., «Искусство», 1955 («Гос. Эрмитаж. Путеводитель по выставке»)

«Русский художественный металл». М., Всесоюзное кооперативное издательство, 1958

Савваитов Павел. Описание старинных русских утварей, одежд, оружия, ратных доспехов и конского прибора в азбучном порядке расположенное. СПб., 1896

Сборник Оружейной палаты. М., 1925

Смирнова Е. И., Шумилов В. Н. Коллекция английского серебра в Оружейной палате Кремля.— «Вопросы архивоведения». М., 1961, № 1

Соболев Н. Н. Русский орнамент. Камень. Дерево. Керамика. Железо. Стенопись. Набойка. М., Гос. архитектурное изд-во, 1948

Спицын А. А. К вопросу о Мономаховой шапке.— «Записки отделения русской и славянской археологии Русского археологического общества», т. 8, вып. I, 1906

Толстой И., Кондаков Н. Русские древности в памятниках искусства, вып. 4—6. СПб., 1891—1899

Троицкий В. И. Организация золотого и серебряного дела в Москве в XVII в.— «Исторические записки», № 12, 1941

Троицкий В. И. Словарь «Мастера-художники золотого и серебряного дела, алмазники, сусальники, работавшие в Москве при Патриаршем дворе в XVII в.» — «Записки Московского Археологического института», т. 36. М., 1914

Троицкий В. И. Словарь московских мастеров золотого, серебряного и алмазного дела XVII в. М.— Л., 1930

Трутовский В. К. Боярин и оружничий Богдан Матвеевич Хитрово и Московская Оружейная палата.— «Старые годы», 1909, июль — сентябрь

Успенский А. И. Столбцы бывшего архива Оружейной палаты. М., 1912

Фелькерзам А. Е. Описи серебра двора его императорского величества. СПб., 1907

Фехнер М. В. Торговля русского государства со странами Востока в XVI в. Труды ГИМ, изд. 2. М., 1956

Филимонов Г. Д. О времени происхождения знаменитой «шапки Мономаха». Чтения в обществе истории и древностей, т. II, 1897

Филимонов Г. Д. Полный хронологический указатель всех марок на серебре московской Оружейной палаты. X том. «Описи московской Оружейной палаты». М., 1893

Флетчер Дж. О государстве Русском. СПб., 1911

«Художественное серебро XVI—XX вв.» Государственный Эрмитаж. Путеводители по выставкам. М., «Искусство», 1956

«Художественные сокровища России», № 9—10, 1902

«Художественные памятники Московского Кремля» (Сборник). М., «Искусство», 1956

Шарая Н. М., Моисеенко Е. Ю. «Костюм в России XVIII — начала XX в. из фондов музея». Каталог. Л., 1962

Scheffler W. Goldschmiede Niedersachsens. 1—2. Berlin. 1965

Штаден Генрих. «О Москве Ивана Грозного». Записки немца опричника. М., Сабашниковы, 1925

Якунина Л. И. Русское шитье жемчугом. М., «Искусство», 1955

INDEX OF NAMES

Armlets of Metropolitan Alexius of Moscow — 27, 28
Arquebuses — 83, 84, 85, 86
Arras — 166, 167
"Baidana" of Tsar Boris Godunov — 60, 61
"Bakhterets" of Tsar Mikhail Feodorovich — 81
"Barmy" of Grand Princes — 3
Basins
— made by Tobias Kramer — 144
— made in France — 154
— made in England — 159
Battle-axes and battle-picks — 62
Boar-spear of Tver Prince Boris Alexandrovich — 9, 10, 11
Bowl of Tsar Alexei Mikhailovich — 114
Bowls and plates — 109, 110, 111, 112
"Bratina"
— of Dyak Mikhail Danilovich — 100
— of Tsar Mikhail Feodorovich — 103
Broadswords — 131
Caps of State
— Diamond Cap of State of Tsar Peter the Great — 97
— Monomachos Cap of State — 128, 129
Censers
— of Prince Yuri Vassilievich — 18
— of Tsarins Irina — 69
Cerement — 77
"Chaldars"
— of Tsar Mikhail Feodorovich — 82
— made in 17th century — 137
Chalices
— of Prince Yuri Dolgoruky — 13
— of Archbishop Moses of Novgorod — 20
— of Tsarina Irina — 70
— made in late 17th century — 142
— made by Andrea Arditi — 149
Coaches
— of Patriarch Philaret — 151
— of Empress Elizaveta Petrovna — 164
Infant coaches of Tsar Peter the Great — 126
"Kolymaga" of Tsar Boris Godunov — 152
Coach Hall Interior — 145
— — 175

Crosses
— made in 1562 — 67
— made in 1636 — 105
Dippers
— of Tsar Mikhail Feodorovich — 101
— of Tsar Mikhail Feodorovich — 102
Disches
— of Tsarina Maria Temryukovna — 64
— made in Holland — 165
Dresses
Caftan — 135
Caftans and camisoles of Emperor Peter II — 160, 161, 162, 163
Grand Robes of State of Tsar Mikhail Feodorovich — 96
"Platno" of Tsar Peter the Great — 127
Coronation robe of Empress Catherine the Great — 168
Coronation robes — 174
Wedding gown of Empress Catherine II — 169
Endova of Boyard Vassili Streshnev — 106
Ewers
— made c. 400 A. D. — 38, 39, 40, 41
— for hand-washing ("voronok") — 153
— made in France — 156
— made by Jean Odiot — 157
Glass — 107
Gospels
— of Metropolian Simon of Moscow — 21, 22
— "Morozov" Gospels — 29, 30, 31, 32
— of Ivan the Terrible — 65
— of Ivan the Terrible — 72
— made in 1678 — 117, 118, 119, 120, 121
Goblet — 143
Gun-"tyufiak" of Tsar Alexei Mikhailovich — 89
Gunner alams — 90, 91
Helmets
— of Prince Yaroslav Vsevolodovich — 1, 2
— with iron-clad necklace — 8
— with "The Deesis" — 36, 37
— made by Lucio Piccinino — 147, 148
Holster — 98
Icons
— "The Virgin Eleusa" — 16, 17

—— "Christ Blessing" 42

—— "Christ Blessing" 43

—— "St Demetrius of Thessalonica" 47

—— "The Virgin Enthroned" 48

—— "St John the Forerunner" 49, 50

—— "St John Climacus" 68

—— "Christ Almighty" 71

—— "The Trinity" 115

—— "The Virgin of Vladimir" with twelve Church Feasts 122

Mountings
—— of icon "The Virgin of Vladimir" 12

—— of icon "The Virgin of Vladimir" ("Photius" mounting) 51

Pall for sepulchre of Metropolitan Jonah of Moscow 123

Panagias
—— made in 15th century 19

—— of Patriarch Job 66

—— of Patriarch Joasaph 11, 113

—— made in 1767 172

Phelonions
—— made in late 16th—early 17th century 76

—— made in 17th century 125

—— made in 1770 173

Pistols 88

"Pokrovets"
—— of Tsar Boris Godunov's horse 73

—— of "saadak" from Grand Robes of State of Tsar Mikhail Feodorovich 92, 93

—— made in 16th century 134

"Prapor" of Vladimir Regiments of Russian Army 87

Reliquaries
Great Zion 14, 15

Philotheus' Staurothèque 46

Shrine 52, 53, 54

"Saadaks"
—— from Grand Robes of State of Tsar Mikhail Feodorovich 94, 95

—— of Tsar Alexei Mikhailovich 138

Saddles
—— of Tsar Boris Godunov 73

—— of Tsar Mikhail Feodorovich 82

—— of Tsar Alexei Mikhailovich 137

Iranian saddles and horse-clothes 136

West-European saddles and horse-clothes 146

Sakkoses
—— of Metropolitan Alexius of Moscow 23, 24, 25

—— of Metropolitan Peter of Moscow 55

—— of Metropolitan Photius of Moscow ("Major" sakkos) 56, 57

—— of Metropolitan Photius of Moscow ("Minor" sakkos) 58, 59

—— of Metropolitan Dionysius of Moscow 74

—— of Metropolitan Anthony of Moscow 75

—— of Patriarch Nicon 78

—— of Patriarch Pitirim 116

—— made in 17th century 139

—— of Patriarch Adrian 150

—— of Patriarch Parthenius of Constantinople 155

Shield of Boyard Feodor Mstislavsky 130

Shrouds
—— "St Demetrius of Thessalonica" 34, 35

—— Puchezha shroud of Christ 33

Small icons
—— "St Demetrius of Thessalonica" 4

—— "The Crucifixion with Interceding Saints" 44

—— "The Descent into Hell" 45

Snuff-boxes
—— made in 1780 170

—— made in 1764 171

Standard of Yermak Timofeevich 63

Stoles
—— of Metropolitan Alexius of Moscow 26

—— made in 17th century 124

Surplice 158

"Tarel" 108

Thrones
—— of Tsar Boris Godunov 132

—— of Tsar Alexei Mikhailovich 133

Tournament armour 140, 141

Trappings of ceremonial horse 99

Triptychs
—— with icon "The Virgin Eleusa" 104

—— made by Lucian 5, 6, 7

"Zertsalos" of Tsar Alexei Mikhailovich 79, 80

C O N T E N T S

PREFACE
BY E. I. SMIRNOVA

RUSSIAN ART OF 12TH-15TH CENTURIES
INTRODUCTORY ARTICLE BY L. V. PISSARSKAYA
PLATES 1—35

BYZANTINE ART OF 5TH-15TH CENTURIES
INTRODUCTORY ARTICLE BY L. V. PISSARSKAYA
PLATES 36—59

RUSSIAN ART OF 16TH CENTURY
INTRODUCTORY ARTICLE BY N. V. GORDEEV
PLATES 60—78

RUSSIAN ART OF 17TH CENTURY
INTRODUCTORY ARTICLE BY L. P. KIRILLOVA
PLATES 79—127

IRANIAN AND TURKISH ART OF 13TH-17TH CENTURIES
INTRODUCTORY ARTICLE BY A. A. GONCHAROVA
PLATES 128—139

WEST-EUROPEAN ART OF 15TH-19TH CENTURIES
INTRODUCTORY ARTICLE BY G. A. MARKOVA
PLATES 140—165

RUSSIAN ART OF 18TH-19TH CENTURIES
INTRODUCTORY ARTICLE BY K. V. DONOVA
PLATES 166—175

COMMENTARY

BIOGRAPHICAL NOTES

GLOSSARY

BIBLIOGRAPHY

INDEX OF NAMES

ALBUM

THE STATE ARMOURY IN THE MOSCOW KREMLIN *(IN ENGLISH)*

Texts by

ALEXANDRA ALEKSEEVNA GONCHAROVA
NIKOLAI VASSILIEVICH GORDEEV
KIRA VLADIMIROVNA DONOVA
LYUBOV PAVLOVNA KIRILLOVA
GALINA ANATOLIEVNA MARKOVA
LYUDMILA VASSILIEVNA PISSARSKAYA
YEVGENIYA IVANOVNA SMIRNOVA

Comments: *96, 97, 127, 128, 129, 132, 133, 160, 161, 162, 163, 166, 167, 168, 169, 174 by A. Goncharova; 1, 2, 8, 9, 10, 11, 36, 37, 60, 61, 62, 63, 79, 80, 81, 83, 84, 85, 86, 87, 88, 89, 90, 91, 92, 93, 94, 95, 130, 131, 138, 140, 141, 147, 148 by N. Gordeev, 23, 24, 25, 26, 27, 28, 33, 34, 35, 55, 56, 57, 58, 59, 74, 75, 76, 77, 78, 116, 122, 123, 124, 125, 139, 150, 155, 158, 170, 171, 172, 173, by* K. Donova *; 73, 82, 98, 99, 126, 134, 136, 137, 151, 152, 164, 175 by L. Kirillova; 142, 143, 144, 145, 146, 149, 153, 154, 156, 157, 159, 165 by G. Markova; 3, 4, 5, 6, 7, 12, 13, 14, 15, 16, 17, 18, 19, 20, 21, 22, 29, 30, 31, 32, 38, 39, 40, 41, 42, 43, 44, 45, 46, 47, 48, 49, 50, 51, 52, 53, 54, 64, 65, 66, 67, 68, 69, 70, 71, 72, 100, 101, 102, 103, 104, 105, 106, 107, 108, 109, 110, 111, 112, 113, 114, 115, 117, 118, 119, 120, 121, by L. Pissarskaya*

Bibliography and text on the jacket *by E. Smirnova*

Album model and design by
YEVGENI ALEXANDROVICH GANNUSHKIN

Photography by
OLGA VSEVOLODOVNA IGNATOVICH AND BORIS VSEVOLODOVICH IGNATOVICH

Translated into English by
ALEXANDRA ILYINICHNA ILF *(Legends, commentary, glossary, index of names)* and
NATASHA JOHNSTONE *(preface, introductory articles, biographical notes)*

Managing editor
ZINAIDA PROKHOROVNA CHELYUBEEVA

Editor of the English text
ALEXANDRA ILYINICHNA ILF

Technical editor
MARGARITA LEONIDOVNA VINOGRADOVA

«Изобразительное искусство» Москва 1969. Стр. 1—216.

Подписано к печати 2/I 1969 г. Изд. № 13—322.
Формат 70 × 108¹/₈. Бумага мелованная и офсетная. Заказ 2232.
Печ. л. 27. Уч.-изд. л. 37,56. Тираж 10 000.

Матрицы изготовлены в 1-ой Образцовой тип. им. А. А. Жданова,
Москва, Ж-54, Валовая, 28

Изготовлено в ГДР